98

HEARTS AND MINDS

The Controversy over Laboratory Animals

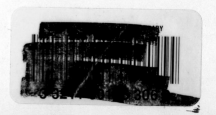

In the series
ANIMALS, CULTURE, AND SOCIETY
edited by
Clinton R. Sanders
and
Arnold Arluke

Hearts

AND

MINDS

The Controversy over Laboratory Animals

Julian McAllister Groves

TEMPLE UNIVERSITY PRESS

Philadelphia

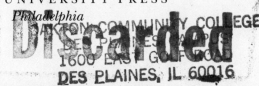

Temple University Press, Philadelphia 19122
Copyright © 1997 by Temple University. All rights reserved
Published 1997
Printed in the United States of America

⊛ The paper used in this book meets the requirements of the American
National Standard for Information Sciences — Permanence of Paper for
Printed Library Materials, ANSI Z39.49-1984
Text design by Gary Gore

Library of Congress Cataloging-in-Publication Data

Groves, Julian McAllister.
    Hearts and minds : the controversy over laboratory animals /
Julian McAllister Groves.
        p.   cm. — (Animals, culture, and society)
    Includes bibliographical references and index.
    ISBN 1-56639-475-9 (alk. paper). — ISBN 1-56639-476-7 (pbk. :
alk. paper)
        1. Animal experimentation — Moral and ethical aspects. 2. Animal
    experimentation — Social aspects. 3. Animal rights. 4. Animal
    rights activists.   I. Title.   II. Series
    R853.A53G76   1997
    174′.28 — dc20   96-7619

Contents

Contents

Preface

In the past twenty years, philosophers, ethicists, and journalists have written extensively about the human treatment of animals. Some of them have advocated that animals should have rights similar to those of humans. Others have justified their use in biomedical research. Ranging from philosophical treatises to exposés of animal abuse and scientific quackery to practical guidelines for treating animals in ethical ways, these writings all refer to a body of formal, consistent moral prescriptions about how people should behave responsibly toward the natural world: Do we have the right to eat animals or use them for our entertainment in zoos? Can we justify using them as subjects in biomedical research? Do animals have rights similar to those of humans?

In this book, however, I am not so much concerned with how people should feel about animals in research. Rather, I am interested in how they do feel about it, why they feel the way they do, and how they feel about their feelings. I am interested in ethics as they are actually practiced by animal rights advocates and animal research supporters in their everyday lives, rather than with ethics as an abstract body of laws. And my focus is on the ordinary people in a small town who make up the rank and file on both sides of the debate, rather than the nationally known leaders and philosophers.

This book would not have been possible without the animal rights activists, animal researchers, and their supporters who volunteered their time to talk with me and allowed me to attend their meetings. Many of them did so believing that they might be putting themselves or their organizations at risk. Their fears are, in part, the story of this book. Nonetheless, except for the nationally known speakers and organizations who intended to disseminate their views to the public, I use pseudonyms to protect the anonymity of the people, places, and organizations I write about, and I have also changed some minor details about certain informants and events.

Part of my research was funded by a grant from the National Science Foundation Program in Ethics and Values (DIR-9121305). Peter Bearman, Judith Blau, Craig Calhoun, Kimberly Chang, Harold Herzog, James Jasper, Sherryl Kleinman, Anthony Oberschall, Clinton Sanders, and Jerome Witschger commented on early drafts. Janet Francendese at Temple University Press gave me the benefit of her experience and patience in finishing the final draft, and Debby Stuart generously provided fine editorial comments. I have also been fortunate to have had friends and students who, in one way or another, have supported my work throughout graduate school and during my stay in Hong Kong: Domio Chow, Jay Goldring, David Lawrence, Suresh Nair, Gerald Patchell, Phoebe, and Mom, who read the proofs with me. Thank you.

Most of all, I am indebted to Arnold Arluke for his encouragement and faith in my work.

HEARTS AND MINDS

The Controversy over Laboratory Animals

Introduction

Shame

We live in a time of unprecedented wealth and comfort. The cold war has ended and nuclear arsenals have been cut. Political and civil rights are no longer restricted by race and gender. We can expect to live over twice as long as we did a hundred years ago, and we have a third more calories available to us than our Third World counterparts. Our work has become more flexible than it used to be. We enjoy faster and easier travel. "Right now," *Rolling Stone* columnist P. J. O'Rourke harks, "at the end of the second millennium, is the best moment of all time, and right here, in the United States, is the best moment to be at that moment."[1]

Yet, O'Rourke and other popular writers see in the mass media a message of dis-ease and dissatisfaction. "I hear America whining, crybaby to the world." We have our comforts, but we seem unable to enjoy them. Why?

Social scientists and other commentators popularly blame "fashionable worries," such as environmental catastrophe, nuclear annihilation, and Third World poverty on the attention-seeking individuals who voice them, politicians who sponsor them, and media-mongers who transmit

1

them. There is some truth to the claim that we have become a society of "professional worrywarts." But what is missing from this account is an understanding of the subjective meanings and emotions that have led us to feel bad about the good life. This book is about such emotions. It is also about the three years I spent with protesters and defenders of animal experimentation in a college town in the southern United States.

Those in favor of animal research believe that animal experimentation is in most cases the only way to learn about human diseases and therapies. Animal rights activists, however, argue that it is morally indefensible to use animals in research because in some ways animals are similar to humans. They have feelings and interests, but they are vulnerable. This makes them worthy of moral protection, regardless of their benefits to humans. In this view, moral distinctions between humans and animals are arbitrary. Humans are animals too.

But underlying these different opinions are feelings common to most of us in our relationship with nature and other consumables that make our modern lifestyles possible. The animal rights activists I have met feel guilty about how they harm animals in their everyday lives through the food they eat, the clothes they wear, the products they use, the entertainment they enjoy, and the medicine they depend on. Most of all, they feel ashamed about exploiting animals when they believe that, as human beings, they have the power to do otherwise. In time I came to understand that many of those who undertake and defend animal research against the animal rights activists also feel guilt and shame over using animals. The killing of animals in medical research is not taken lightly. It is shrouded in rituals and regulations and justified by arguments about the benefits of animal research for improving both human and animal lives. Animal rights activists and animal researchers alike acknowledge the moral cost of using animals. Both groups are forced to deal with the guilt and shame that goes with it. This book is the story of how each side does so.

Shame and Pride

Emotions underlie social conflict, but sociologists shy away from this most basic fact. There are good reasons for this. Since Plato, intellectuals have contrasted emotions with reason, fact with value.[2] From this perspective, emotions are the unexplainable or irrational part of human behavior. As social scientists, we rarely examine our own feelings about those we study,[3] and so it is not surprising that we neglect those of others. Participants in the so-called New Social Movements, sociologists tell us, seek not just money and power but a feeling: a sense of personal worth or collective identity. They want to feel good about being black, gay, male, or female. They are in an "identity quest."[4] But writers on these movements avoid all specific mention of basic emotions like guilt and shame that come from a spoiled identity, and rarely do we see chapters devoted to pride and honor.[5] Instead, they look at how emotions are driven by ideology, not the other way around. They describe emotions as constructed, not as felt; as instruments of manipulation and intrigue, not as indicators of anxiety or strain.

People do feel. They do not just imagine their emotions. Psychologists and psychiatrists have long recognized this. Their theories about emotions have been incorporated by one neglected sociologist who writes about social conflict, Thomas Scheff. Scheff has developed a theory that focuses specifically on the emotional dynamics in conflicts — conflicts that range from marital squabbles to international political crises and wars.[6]

Protracted conflicts, according to Scheff, arise from the fundamental emotion of shame. But shame is actually only an indicator of a much broader problem in our relationships. We feel ashamed when we have been rejected or isolated by others. We may also feel ashamed for the opposite reason. Sometimes we are so enmeshed in our relationships, so connected with others, that we feel ashamed when we violate their expectations of us, or when they violate our expectations of them.

Our society represses shame. In English, there are few words to express this complex emotion, whereas other cultures distinguish between several different types of shame. Some of these are even pleasurable. Germans, for instance, use the word *Scham* to name an everyday kind of shame that suggests modesty or shyness. Shame in our language is a purely dark and negative emotion. Our avoidance of shame is such that we usually speak about it in euphemisms: "I was embarrassed," "It was an awkward situation."[7] Words such as *upset, anger,* and *hurt* often substitute for shame. Sometimes we respond to shame by saying nothing at all.[8] The Chinese, in contrast, talk about shame all the time and are openly concerned about protecting others from humiliation by allowing them to "save face." In the West we learn from an early age to disguise our shame. We tend to transmute it to other more acceptable emotions such as pride, self-confidence, and anger.

According to Scheff, when we fail to acknowledge our shame, protracted conflict occurs. In these situations, shame perpetuates itself. We become ashamed about being ashamed. Eventually, we may become angry at being ashamed. Nowhere is this more apparent than in the public world of international affairs. The Treaty of Versailles following the First World War, for example, made ordinary German citizens feel rejected and therefore shamed before the international community. Germans actually referred to it as the "Treaty of Shame." Hitler's popularity rested on his ability to offer Germans alternatives to shame and its related emotions: "Instead of anomie, Hitler offered community," Scheff points out, "and instead of humiliation, pride and self-confidence."[9]

Studies of Hitler's personality—from his sex life to his writings in *Mein Kampf*—reveal that he himself was plagued with shame. He enjoyed degrading sexual acts, such as being urinated on. He dwelt on the humiliation of Germany's defeat and disarmament. Yet he often hid this shame in pride. As the arguments in his autobiography unfold, talk of shame turns quickly to "self-confidence," "faith in invincibility," and "superiority to others." And then it turns to aggression: "Give us arms again!" In explaining the protracted conflict that led to the Second World War, Scheff describes a "triple spiral of shame-rage." Hitler and his followers were ashamed, but they were also angry about having to be ashamed and ashamed about being angry. They were caught in a "shame-rage feeling trap."[10] Instead of condemning or ignoring Germany's shame, Hitler displayed it in himself. He helped German citizens mitigate their shame by showing them how to be proud. He did this, in part, by attributing their shame to Jews. He was essentially telling Germans: "You needn't be ashamed of being humiliated and enraged; it's not your fault."[11]

Scheff's study of the shame-rage spiral helps us understand how leaders appeal to the public. The secret of charisma, Scheff suggests, lies in finding ways to identify with and then mitigate the shame levels of one's followers. Ronald Reagan's charisma, for instance, came from his open expressions of insult and outrage and hints of retaliation in international crises, such as the Iranian hostage-taking of Americans. This eventually led to military action, such as the bombing of Tripoli. Reagan's predecessor, Jimmy Carter, was less successful in this respect. Although he spoke of preserving honor, Carter seldom expressed emotion, and when he did, it came out in less forceful words like "discomfiture." Using a language of restraint rather than retaliation made Carter look weak and indecisive in the eyes of voters. Politicians face a dilemma: They lose charisma if they resist the shame-rage spiral, but they endanger their solidarity with and stability in the international community if they give in to it.[12]

Shame was a recurrent theme in my interviews with animal rights activists and animal researchers. In a debate I heard between proponents on a local radio station, a journalist sympathetic to both sides pointed out: "The only reason we're even debating this is that our brains have evolved to the point where we're ashamed of our place in the food chain." Although the word *shame* is not always explicit, descriptions of guilt over using animals hint at this emotion.

Guilt and shame are not the same. We normally reserve the word *guilt* for how we feel when we have broken a rule. Shame is a more devastating attack on our whole person. When we feel ashamed, we feel totally inferior, degraded, or exposed.[13] Guilt and shame, however, often occur together. Psychologists have shown that these emotions emerge at about the same age in children.[14] Guilt and shame intertwine in what psychiatrist Léon Wurmser calls a "guilt/shame dialectic." In the Vietnam War, for instance, foreign critics said that it was shameful for a powerful nation like the United States to wage war against a weaker one. Antiwar protesters and veterans internalized this shame and experienced feelings of guilt about specific attacks on innocent civilians. These feelings were the source of more shame. If America was supposed to be an international leader in justice, democracy, and self-determination, how could its citizens feel guilty?[15]

Animal rights literature reminds activists of their guilt over how they treat animals and offers them a way to mitigate it by showing them how to lead cruelty-free lives. Like other protest movements, the animal rights movement gives its followers a sense of control in situations in which they would normally feel powerless. Animal rights activists embrace an ethic of personal responsibility. They learn how their actions help animals, whether by becoming a vegetarian, taking part in protests, or educating the public.

Adopting an alternative lifestyle presented a dilemma for the animal rights activists I followed. Although it helped alleviate their shame, it did so by shaming others. It brought them into direct conflict with those who did not lead cruelty-free lives. No one likes to be thought of as an animal abuser. This conflict isolated the activists from the mainstream of society, particularly from professionals such as scientists, whose status many wanted to emulate. Some activists felt ashamed by their emotions. They were ashamed not only about using animals but also about being ashamed.

The research establishment responded to its shame differently. Rather than publicly acknowledging it, they transmuted it to pride — pride in medical advancements through animal research. Pride is the counterpart of shame.[16] There cannot be pride unless there is shame, since one usually acts proud in order to hide one's shame. In an attempt to persuade the public, research supporters highlighted their heroic attempts to manage nature, and they argued that the animal rights activists were responsible for human and animal suffering. But this pride had consequences. It made animal rights activists appear "anti-science" while making researchers look arrogant and elitist. Like animal rights activists, researchers were caught in their own feeling traps. They were ashamed about cruelty in animal research. They were angry about having to be ashamed, and ashamed about being angry.

Shame Movements

Shame and pride are only part of the story. Modern sentiments toward animals have evolved slowly as a result of large-scale social changes such as industrialization and urbanization. Our feelings about animals are also the result of a long socialization process that begins in childhood with the help of children's books and films about animals, television programs about nature, and high school biology classes. Animal protection has become a symbol of civility for advanced industrial nations.

The residents of the college town in which I lived and write about here saw themselves enmeshed in shameful relationships, aside from their use of animals. The town boasts an elite, prestigious university system, medical schools, and pharmaceutical and other research corporations. The town and the surrounding areas, however, still bear the scars of a colonial past of slavery, working-class poverty, and rapid, sometimes uncontrolled development. This shame expressed itself in the civil rights movement of the 1960s, when the state was home to some of the earliest protests against segregation in the United States, and now in a more prevalent movement for multiculturalist values. What is multiculturalism if not a movement that reminds us of our shameful colonial past and then bestows this shame upon others, the utterers of "politically incorrect" words and ideas? Animal rights activists draw frequent parallels between the civil rights movement and their own. Environmentalism is also prevalent in the town. Although the philosophy of environmentalism is different from that of the animal rights movement, its followers find in it ways to mitigate their guilt and shame too. "We have wished, we ecofreaks," writes Stewart Brand in the *Whole Earth Catalogue*, "for a disaster or for a social change to come and bomb us into the Stone Age, where we might live like Indians in our Valley, with our localism, our appropriate technology, our gardens, our homemade religion — guilt-free

at last!"[17] Guilt and its related sentiment shame are emotions whose time has come for animals in this college town
community, and in others like it.

Social movement organizations, with the help of the
media, mobilize the shame already within us and then
transmute it to more manageable emotions of pride, anger, or empowerment. What sociologists call "framing"
moves the process along. Like the frame on a painting, the
metaphorical frames promoted by social movements tell us
what we need to pay attention to. They tell us what problems need to be addressed, who is responsible for them,
and what should be done about them.[18] They provide, if
you like, the moral fix. They do so by disseminating their
views through the media. In this multimedia sociey, we can
feel guilt and shame about our relationships with peoples
remote from us. In the Global Village, anyone can be our
neighbor. *The Economist,* for instance, aptly described the
war in Bosnia as a "crisis of conscience" in the international community. Media stories of ethnic cleansing and
women being raped by Serb aggressors in the faces of helpless Western peacekeepers and diplomats created "a widespread sense of shame, and weakness, in the West."[19] Finding ourselves backing the losing side, we lost our credibility
and turned to military action to restore it.

It is not true, then, that we have fully repressed our guilt
and shame. Many social movements are explicitly about
these feelings. To be sure, we live in a rationalized society, in
which we frequently value the nonemotional persona. But
precisely because we live in a rationalized society, this is also
an age in which we value personal expression. Where our
increasingly service-oriented society requires us to put on

acts, to smile for the customer, to wear a different hat for a
different occasion; where we are increasingly known only by
our specialized roles and job titles; and where media repre-
sentations of reality are often mistaken for reality itself, our
personal feelings and intuition have become symbols of
authenticity, sincerity, and our "true selves."[20]

It has become particularly fashionable for some groups
to express their shame or at least humility. After the Reagan
and Thatcher years of self-interest and thrift, politicians
began to speak of a "kinder, gentler nation." Courses in
ethics and values proliferated in business and professional
schools. Centers and institutes were dedicated to studying
and promoting values in science, technology, and public
policy.[21] Feminists argued for a morality based on sensitivity
and cooperation rather than on abstract principles and
competition.[22] The film industry turned Arnold Schwarze-
negger from policeman to kindergarten teacher, and from
stoic scientist to weepy expectant mother. The passing of
fifty years since the Nazi Holocaust and reports of recent
human atrocities in the former Yugoslavia have encouraged an international debate over whether alleged perpetrators of war crimes have expressed enough remorse for
what they did.[23] We have become not just ashamed about
being ashamed but proud of being ashamed.

But the rules for this emotional expression do not apply
equally to everyone. Women pay a higher price than men
for taking part in the expressive movement. When a man is
caring or humble—as depicted in posters of half-naked,
muscular men holding babies—he is likely to be praised.
A recent advertisement for Philips shavers urges men to
"shave with care," because "showing your feelings is not a

sign of weakness, it's a sign of strength." The opposite is also true. What can be more impressive than a man's anger? Robert Bly, the influential writer in the men's movement, encourages men to get in touch with the "Wild Man" that lurks at the bottom of their psyches. The Wild Man, Bly reminds us, is not to be confused with the Savage. In an age in which corporations produce "sanitized, hairless, shallow men," the Wild Man is receptive and expressive.[24]

Women, however, are less likely to be praised for being caring or angry. Their emotions are often seen as irrational. Professional women feel threatened when their work becomes expressive because to some it seems less legitimate. In *Equals Before God*, sociologist Sherryl Kleinman describes women entering the ministry as cynical about training that encourages "womanly values," such as egalitarianism, cooperation, and expressiveness. The women she interviewed wanted "intellectual" and "theological" justifications for women's participation in the ministry. They believed that the minister's authority rests on male status, not womanly feelings.[25]

This resistance is going on in the broader American educational system. The growth of liberal arts and multicultural programs in U.S. colleges has encouraged a view that knowledge is subjective and intuitive; that women's and minorities' opinions carry equal validity to those of mainstream thinkers. But some women resist what they regard as romantic relativism. In *Women's Ways of Knowing*, Mary Field Belenky and her collegues show that women in elite colleges continue to believe that, at least in their art classes, their teachers demand not just personal opinions but the procedures by which they arrived at them: "composition and texture and 'all that garbage.' " The students learned that "intuitions may deceive; that gut reactions can be irresponsible and no one's gut feeling is infallible; that some truths are truer than others; that they can know things they have never seen or touched; that truth can be shared; and that expertise can be respected."[26]

Some women who regard themselves as feminists have rejected traditional ideas about femininity as well as, for instance, sexual harassment laws and other forms of legislation to protect women. These, they argue, reinforce a view of women as helpless victims in need of paternal protection.[27] The "postmodern feminists" go as far as to argue that we must no longer focus on categories such as male and female; we must move away from the idea that there are male and female ways of thinking and looking at the world. Such categories, they say, only reinforce sexism because the women's view will always be regarded as inferior.[28]

Animal rights activists face a similar dilemma. Women dominated the early animal protection movements. Animals, along with children, became objects of compassion and part of the home and family. Animal protectionism, like the temperance and peace movements, offered these women a way to participate in public life at a time when men excluded them from other aspects of it. The recent animal rights movement has also been described as a "moral crusade" that criticizes the rational, calculating attitude of businessmen and scientists in favor of an ethic of caring and responsibility—a leftover of the romanticism of the 1960s.[29]

Many of the career-minded women I met in the animal rights movement believed, however, that being associated with compassion limits opportunities rather than expands them. Such women know what it means when a female senator dissolves in tears while taking part in a public debate, or when they feel tears of anger welling during an argument at work, as they did when they appeared before television cameras to talk about animal cruelty: "Emotions don't win arguments." These animal rights activists believed that they had to find "rational" ways to be emotional about animals. The animal rights movement is made up predominantly of women. But among the animal rights activists I got to know, men, whom the activists saw as less "emotional," were more charismatic.

Those who support animal research face the opposite challenge. Popular images of scientists portray them as detached and inhuman at a time when it is unpopular for professionals to be so. Those who organize to defend animal research believe that to win public support they must show their compassion for animals. In the words of one research proponent: "Be a human first, a scientist second."[30] Pro-research activists rely on mothers with sick children, patient groups, family doctors, and veterinarians, in addition to medical scientists, to support animal research. Whereas animal rights activists rationalize their emotions for animals, pro-researchers emotionalize their rationality.

The animal research controversy is, for me, a microcosm of the guilt and shame that pervades modern relationships. And this does not apply just to those outside the world of industry and commerce: "What Humans Owe to Animals" was the feature article in a recent edition of *The Economist*.[31] Animal rights activists and research supporters represent an extreme case, but they tell us something about ourselves. They have been forced to deal with a dilemma that is common to most of us but resolved by few. No matter how delicately we try to skate upon this earth, our actions have consequences for others, whether they be human or nonhuman. In a multimedia and globalized society, these consequences are more apparent to us now than ever before.

This book is about how concerned citizens in a community dealt with this Buddhist maxim of cause and effect. It is about the very definition of what it means to be a responsible citizen. But above all, it is about how members of a community sought and fought for integration over isolation, acceptance over rejection.

These themes seem strikingly apparent now, but I did not see them when I first became involved with the animal research controversy. This was because, like many social scientists, I tried to gaze at the controversy from a dispassionate position, without attempting to see it in my own life as a nonactivist.

One

The Activists and I

Why, I wondered, would people spend so much time protesting animal research? Did they think lab rats were more important than people? On February 20, 1989, while working as a part-time sociology instructor in a mid-size college town—which I refer to in this book as the College Town—I decided to go to a campus meeting of animal rights activists to find out. The students put me in touch with a statewide organization in which I spent the next three years visiting information tables and attending meetings, protests, vegetarian meals, and social gatherings. Twenty animal rights activists whom I met along the way agreed to sit down with me over a tape recorder and talk about how they became involved with the movement.

Looking back, I see that my questions hinted at my initial cynicism about the animal rights movement. I had invited animal rights activists to construct an elaborate argument for me about why biomedical research is particularly evil compared to other kinds of animal use and why even lab rats deserve special treatment. I came away with a fanciful description of a society that has been led astray by sci-

17

ence, technology, and industrialization: the proverbial Fall from Eden. The end of animal research would herald a new age in which people would live in harmony with nature and one another.

This description was similar to some of the sociological accounts I had already read about the animal rights movement. These suggest that the movement can be explained by the growth of a consistent anti–science, technology, and business attitude.[1] Some critics of the animal rights movement have taken a negative spin on this, declaring that animal rights activists are not sincere about helping animals, that they are only masking an anti-science agenda.[2]

My initial essays reflect this view. Animal rights activists, I wrote, are driven by interests that are above and beyond their concern for animals. To be fair, I portrayed animal researchers equally narrowly. Their interests, I said, are to keep the animal rights activists and the general public out of science so they can maintain their prestige and autonomy. This meshed well with what other sociologists have written about scientists: that they strive to preserve their authority, status, and power by creating boundaries between scientists and laymen, science and pseudo-science.[3]

But how was I to explain the emotional bonds with animals and the altruism that activists on both sides of the controversy profess? Indeed, most animal rights activists are involved in humane or animal protection societies, and many animal researchers pursued biology because they love nature. Science, for them, is a way to help it. I conceded that activists on both sides do feel pity for animals, but I interpreted these feelings merely as social constructs or rhetoric manufactured by the animal rights and animal research supporters. In saying this, I concurred with what many sociologists say about public controversies: that they are purely "dramas" contrived to pull people in, but nothing more.[4]

I looked back at what I had written. By saying that the activists were "constructing" emotions, I seemed to be suggesting that they did not really feel them or that their emotions were not really there. They were a figment of the imagination. I felt cynical again, as if I were one of the commentators who see animal rights activists and animal researchers as furthering their own interests. As field researchers, we are told that we are supposed to see the world as our informants see it, to put ourselves in their shoes.[5] But I was writing an account that I knew both animal rights activists and animal researchers would see as distasteful portrayals of themselves.

It struck me that while being cynical, I had missed something. I had been attending animal rights meetings without really attending to how the animal rights activists actually felt about animal cruelty. Nor was I putting myself in the activists' shoes. By ignoring my own feelings about animal cruelty, I was not letting myself be moved by animal rights literature in the way that animal rights activists were. I recalled in my fieldnotes, for instance, how I became nervous and evasive when informants or even colleagues and friends would ask, "Well, who's side are you on?" To be sure, I felt revulsion and anger when watching animal rights videos about animal research. I also sympathized with animal researchers who were very caring about their animals. But I did not want to admit these feelings openly. Why?

Above all, I knew that whichever side I took would get

me into uncomfortable discussions. Most of the animal rights activists I met had read and thought a lot about animal rights issues, particularly animal research. They could always find an opposing argument. When I debated with them, I felt humiliated, as if I were responsible for animal cruelty by my own ignorance.

I also thought that taking a position would turn the other side against me or my work and deny me access to interviews and meetings. There were good reasons for these concerns. Early in my involvement in the animal rights movement, I learned that some animal rights activists suspected me of being a spy for the animal researchers. I felt that I had to provide them with letters of identification. Animal researchers were even more suspicious about me and what I would write. Elsewhere in the country, animal rights activists, posing as research staff, had dealt cruel blows to animal researchers by "infiltrating" their institutions and painting them and their facilities in a dismal light.[6] Why should researchers trust me?

But it was not just my informants in the controversy that I worried about. I was reluctant to express my feelings and opinions to colleagues and friends. I was worried that they would think that I had been "sucked in" by one side and that my work was biased. I had always been suspicious of colleagues who were studying groups with whom they were involved or sympathetic, such as feminists who studied women's organizations. I suspected that they would use their research to further their personal goals, rather than find sociological "truths," as if these ideals were inseparable.

Finally, I did not want to express my feelings about animal research because I was worried that people would mistake *me* for being an animal rights activist or an animal research sympathizer. I was embarrassed about what these identities entailed. In fact I was embarrassed about the whole issue of animal protection. On one hand I enjoyed the fact that the animal rights movement was a "fringe group" and was often in the news. On the other hand I had a nagging feeling that its popularity was due to its timeliness rather than its timelessness.[7] The animal rights movement appeared to be sporadic, trendy, and frivolous, in contrast to the civil rights movement, the women's movement, or Amnesty International. Even the environmental movement—which does not fight for the rights of people—seemed more important, with its global and political concerns.

I read into others clues about my marginality. I thought that I detected a glazed look on the faces of people who had never thought or heard about animal rights. I recall finding myself making polite conversation at a buffet dinner with a distinguished sociologist; juggling his plate and wineglass in his hands, he urged me to study the larger national organizations rather than student activists, who might make my work look "trivial." A few years later, at a sociology convention, a professor for whom I once worked as a teaching assistant and whom I respected enormously asked me why participant observers usually study "exotic" groups rather than bank clerks. My heart sank. Was the animal rights movement really exotic? Had I become too absorbed with the controversy to realize? And during an interview for a job in Southeast Asia, one interviewer implied to me that animal protection is a Western sensibility, as if people in other cultures do not keep pets.

Accepting that "You are what you study,"[8] I began to find ways to overcome my uneasiness. I would tell people that I was studying "ethics — how people resolve ethical dilemmas." If they probed further, I would say, "Science and ethics — moral dilemmas faced by scientists." Science and ethics, as I mention above, were becoming big issues in the mid-1980s. Only when I was really pressed on the subject would I mutter something about animals. But all along, I was avoiding both my informants' and my own feelings about animal cruelty.

Once I had the more stable job as a full-time lecturer, I began to think again about my feelings in the animal research controversy. I was also influenced by the small number of sociologists who dare to bare all, and to analyze their own feelings in order to analyze those of the people they study.[9] This made me realize that by denying my own feelings I had been missing another story. For a start, I was inadvertently doing exactly what animal rights activists and animal researchers do all the time.

You see, like many animal rights activists, I may have been drawn to the animal rights movement because I myself had always been bothered by the contradiction that we both eat animals and keep them as pets. I was curious to know how other people — people who had really thought about the issue — resolved the dilemma.

It was unusually cold on that February night when I attended my first animal rights meeting in 1989. Light snow had dusted the grassy spots between buildings and had become puckered with rain. I dressed in a down jacket that I had bought for a trip to Chicago a few years earlier. I can still picture that coat, bright blue and hanging on a peg at the back of the church hall where the animal rights activists met. During that meeting and in the months that followed, I, along with the animal rights activists, entered the world of animal cruelty and exploitation through animal rights videos and literature about animal research, fur trapping, and factory farms. I began to feel awkward about bringing that coat to the meetings. I knew where those down feathers had come from and I did not want to know how they got there.

I tried being vegetarian. I got testy when there was no meatless option on the menu at a restaurant or when friends served me meat. I kept thinking about the T-shirt one activist often wore at protests, proclaiming "MEAT STINKS!" in bloody letters. I became aware of animal cruelty that I would normally not have noticed. On a trip to Disney World in Florida with my parents, for instance, all the while I watched the dolphin show, my mind was on how the dolphins were being treated behind the public's view. I became aware of the stale stench of urine outside the psychology department that I biked past every day to work on crisp fall days under a clear sky. I'm here but for the grace of God, I thought. Like the animal rights activists, I felt ashamed at myself for being a part of animal cruelty, for conniving with its perpetrators by not doing more to stop it. I was also ashamed about being ashamed. I wanted to couch my research in terms of science and ethics to give it more importance. Animal rights activists, I realized, were doing the same thing. They too would rather argue against the scientific merits of animal research or talk philosophy than discuss their feelings about animals and animal suffering. Like the animal rights activists, I became angry with the animal researchers. Why, I wondered, were they refusing to let the animal rights activists attend review board meetings to approve or disapprove animal research? Why were they even refusing to let activists see researchers' proposals to do animal research? What were they hiding? These activists were not terrorists. They were ordinary, educated, concerned citizens who appeared to know a lot about science.

That was when I began to interview animal research supporters. I went directly to those responding to the animal rights activists' accusations: senior university administrators, committees that reviewed animal research proposals, organizations that supported animal research, and researchers accused of being cruel to animals. At first, they confirmed the activists' claims. Most of them were reluctant to talk to me. The greatest reluctance came from those I expected to be the most open on the issue, the chairs of the research review committees. I persisted. The chair of one committee began to take an interest in me. Gradually, one by one, he arranged for me to interview each of the committee members. I felt I was winning their trust, and I was confident that by the end of the interviews I would be able to attend their meetings as a full participant observer. But I was wrong. After I had interviewed most of the committee members, the chair still would not let me attend committee's meetings. The other members, he said, did not "feel ready for it." I was shaking with anger about this. In my conversations with them, the committee members had encouraged me to attend the meetings. I had been polite and fair. I was teaching classes on the campus at the time. What did he think I was going to do?

I never did get to attend those meetings. I did, however,

interview several of the participants, as well as university administrators, targeted researchers, and members of pro-research organizations — twenty people in all. I conducted some of these interviews in the College Town. Others I conducted at a government research institute in a neighboring research park where a friend of mine was doing his Ph.D. research in toxicology. Still other interviews I conducted in a larger city twenty miles from the College Town where animal rights activists were targeting Rachel Rosenthal, a neuroscientist who experimented on cats. Back in the College Town, I accompanied the research review committee on its biannual inspection of the animal holding facilities and shadowed the university veterinarian in his meetings with his staff of animal caretakers and technicians.

After a while, I began to soften toward these people. I did not like seeing the animals in cages, but they did not appear to suffer in the way that animal rights literature said that they did. The dog pens at the university reminded me of the ones at the humane society shelter where many animal rights activists work as volunteers. Some research review committee members clearly struggled with aspects of animal research. They had read some of the philosophical writings on animal rights that the animal rights activists read. They agonized over whether to allow certain experiments. They also appeared willing to violate institutional and federal regulations in order to protect the animals from unnecessary cruelty.

There was one researcher, an immunologist I call Henry Weiss, whom I particularly liked. A middle-aged, avuncular man, he spoke so quickly in a high-pitched voice that I had to tape record everything he said for fear I would lose it. He was animated by the issues. He would tell amusing and endearing stories about working with animals, and he challenged his superiors about how lab animals should be treated. Once he adopted a goat as a pet rather than have it euthanized at the end of his experiments. Keeping lab animals as pets was forbidden, and so he told the administrators that the animal had gone to "goat heaven." He could have lost his job over this. He welcomed the comments and opinions of animal rights activists — something all the other committee members I spoke to refused to consider. He even persuaded the university veterinarian, against the recommendations of his colleagues, to allow animal rights activists to walk the laboratory dogs, but the animal rights activists did not show up for the first session. Weiss lost face over this.

Now I was beginning to get angry with the animal rights activists. They were not willing to work with the researchers in making conditions better for the animals. Instead, they publicly humiliated them. I also felt foolish for having been taken in by my emotions — emotions that the animal rights activists had encouraged in me. I could still care about animals, I rationalized, and live with some kinds of animal research, provided that it was supervised by these nice researchers. I did not want to tell this to the animal rights activists, however, for some of the reasons I mentioned earlier; I thought they would humiliate and reject me.

Some animal rights activists had had responses similar to mine. Initially, a few could support some animal experiments. They simply opposed using abandoned pets in animal research or wanted to ensure that the lab animals were well cared for. Still, they worried that they were betraying the animals and the animal rights movement if they accepted some animal use but not others. This made them feel inconsistent—a criticism cynics often leveled against them.

I learned two things from these reflections. First, while other writers on the animal rights controversy have expressed their feelings about animal cruelty, they have not used their feelings to understand the activists. In their introduction to *The Animal Rights Movement in America*, Lawrence and Susan Finsen say: "We have not endeavored in this book to hide our position as advocates of animal rights, nor do we think that it would be particularly intellectually honest or desirable. Nonetheless, we have strived for objectivity in our account of the movement and the philosophical ideas that ground it."[10] Such objectivity leads them to focus on the philosophy of the movement, even though animal cruelty involves intense feelings. By taking pains to maintain silence with the knowledge of such cruelty, they tell us something about the significance of their feelings. Similarly, in *Animal Liberators*, Susan Sperling waxes poetic as she describes "being transfixed with sorrow" over the "small beautiful creature" that had "had a life in the field" and "lived out the small passions of a rodent's existence"[11] while she was dissecting a guinea pig in her anthropological research. Instead of analyzing these feelings, she insists that the animal research controversy is about a world "besieged by technology."[12] In effect, she marginalizes the activists' feelings about animal suffering as well as the multiplicity of personal meanings that participating in the movement has in their own lives. As is often true, there is not one story here, but several.

Second, by being openly unsympathetic toward animal rights activists or toward animal researchers, by poking at the apparent irrationality or inconsistencies in their beliefs, one gets a one-dimensional picture of their worlds as they strive to defend them. Like psychologists, one tends to look at activists as having consistent values, thought-worlds, or "personality types."[13] Or like some sociologists, one might see animal rights activists as "militant" or "fundamentalist,"[14] and animal researchers as "controlling,"[15] without understanding the contexts in which they become so. In other words, animal rights activists are often driven to fundamentalist positions when confronted with cynical outsiders who want to point out their inconsistencies. And the same is true for those who support animal research. The positions taken by one side can be understood only by looking at their relationship with the other.[16]

In this book then, I suggest that animal rights activists and animal research supporters are not as different as they have been made out to be with regard to their feelings about animals. In Chapter Two, I examine how animal protection[17] became institutionalized in England and the United States and how this occurred not just among animal rights activists but also among animal researchers.

In Chapter Three, I describe the setting in which I studied the animal research controversy. I want to show that, contrary to popular beliefs and sociological accounts and surveys that portray animal rights activists as anti–science and technology, the situation is more complex. The lives of some of the animal rights followers were embedded in science and technology through their occupations and their regular use of television and computer networks, while some animal research supporters were skeptical of science and support regulating animal experiments.

In Chapters Four and Five, I look at how animal rights activists and animal researchers dealt with their ambivalence about animal use. Animal rights activists embraced an ethic of personal responsibility for their actions. Their response was confessional and individualistic. By contrast, animal researchers and their supporters sought for themselves a protective role in nature through science. They argued for a trust in experts through a division of labor — a Hobbesian solution to the problem of order.

In Chapters Six and Seven, I discuss animal rights activists and animal researchers in the context of the news media and critics in order to explain why the controversy became one about rights for animals and scientific progress, rather than about compassion for pets — as it began. Specifically, I examine animal rights activists' ambivalence toward their emotions over animal cruelty by looking at how they used the term "emotional" to describe one another. I describe how some of them tried to resolve their ambivalence by finding "rational" or "scientific" ways to argue for animal protection. This was sometimes part of a professional or gender strategy to legitimate animal protection in their own eyes and in the eyes of skeptics. Animal researchers, by contrast, embraced emotional public relations campaigns in an attempt to win, in the words of one proponent, both the "hearts and minds" of the public. They turned their shame over animal use into pride in human achievements by portraying researchers as heroic, compassionate, and victimized.

In Chapter Eight, I examine another response to the animal research controversy, the adoption of federal and institutional guidelines for laboratory animal welfare. Far from establishing a rationally based common ground for ethical decision making — as they were designed to do — the guidelines divided the research establishment. Some contradicted researchers' emotional attachments to animals; some interfered with their relationships with animal care staff and administrators; others set up constraints that encouraged researchers to violate regulations, leaving them vulnerable to criticism from animal rights activists.

I conclude with a discussion about interactions between animal rights activists and animal research supporters. I describe how each side in the controversy perpetuated the opposition's isolation and shame, and I suggest how the controversy might have been diffused by reducing the isolation between each party.

Two

The Human Dilemma

The Egyptians worshipped cats. The French burned them for entertainment. The Chinese used them for food. Western social philosophers have shown how we are different from animals. Naturalists have shown how we are similar. Neither fully human nor fully object, animals occupy an ambiguous status in our culture that is open to interpretation.

There is a tendency to think that only those living in affluent societies get sentimental about pets. Yet I suspect that emotional attachments to animals are a universal part of all human cultures. In *Animals and People Sharing the World*, James Serpell describes how European colonialists were astonished to find villages of the native inhabitants "infested with pets of every description." From the Barasana Indians of eastern Colombia to the Dyaks of Borneo, he records accounts of cats, dogs, bears, birds, and other wild animals being tamed, "loved," "fondled," and even breast-fed by the inhabitants.[1] How then, have we tried to come to terms with both sentimentalizing animals and using them for our own subsistence?

Until the eighteenth century, most people in the West

recognized no such contradiction and drew clear boundaries between man and nature.[2] Religious leaders and philosophers justified these boundaries with doctrines that placed people above animals. According to the Old Testament, God gave Adam "dominion" over all living things. The seventeenth-century philosopher Descartes supported this view by pronouncing animals to be machines without minds or souls. Common people took this to mean that animals exist only to serve human whim, no matter how cruel or bizarre. According to Keith Thomas, popular entertainments in seventeenth-century England included throwing ducks into pike-infested ponds and biting the heads off chickens and sparrows. As England became increasingly reliant on animals for fuel and food, people began to believe that animals benefit from and even enjoy sacrificing themselves for humans, as a seventeenth-century country poem suggests:

> *The pheasant, partridge and the lark*
> *Flew to thy house, as to the Ark.*
> *The willing ox of himself came*
> *Home to the slaughter, with the lamb;*
> *And every beast did thither bring*
> *Himself to be an offering.*[3]

But even in those times, there were intellectuals who saw this philosophy as no more than a thinly veiled justification for animal exploitation, a way to appease the conscience over what was obviously animal suffering. In 1648, the theologian Henry More told Descartes frankly that his was a "murderous doctrine."[4]

What happened to change this human-centered uni-

verse such that it was no longer acceptable to see animals in
purely utilitarian terms? Ironically, in the light of the animal research controversy, it was the early modern scientists
who encouraged us to see animals as being similar to humans. In the late seventeenth and early eighteenth centuries, naturalists, such as Andrea Cesalpino and John Ray,
developed taxonomies that no longer classified nature in
terms of its usefulness to humans — its edibility, beauty, or
benevolence — but by its inherent structure and functions.
In 1735 Carolus Linnaeus grouped *Homo sapiens* with primates in the order Anthropomorphia. Other naturalists,
such as John Locke and Gottfried Leibnitz, went further in
challenging the boundaries between humans and animals.
They conceptualized nature as a "chain of being," consist-
ing of minute gradations or even a continuous unbroken
spectrum with no clear lines separating animals from people. Charles Darwin's nineteenth-century theory of man's
evolution from apes reinforced the idea of a continuous
chain of being. The Victorian criminologist Cesare Lom-
broso, arguing that criminals' brains and facial features
resemble those of great apes, encouraged further comparisons between man and beast. In the words of James
Turner, who writes about the history of the animal research
controversy, these pioneering scientists "forced the Vic-
torians to look their animal cousins full in the face," and to
"reckon with the beast."[5]

Women and the Humane Movement

Social and economic changes further dissolved the
moral boundaries between humans and animals. The

growth of cities during England's industrialization in the nineteenth century separated increasing numbers of people from farm life. Frequent trips to the countryside provided an escape from polluted cities. People began to romanticize nature, seeing it as less brutish and more benign. Victorian paintings revealed animals languishing around the house. Animals, like children, were increasingly becoming the objects of sentimentality and adoration, rather than economic assets. They were now part of the family and home — a haven to which the middle classes were retreating from industrial life.

By most accounts, animal protection was a women's movement — an extension of women's growing role as society's caretakers.[6] In Victorian England, men excluded women from the public world of industry and politics. Taking what was left for themselves, women in the middle and upper classes defined the private world of homemaking as their own.[7] Against the harshness of factory life and working-class poverty, they promoted kindness and compassion for the weak and vulnerable — children, the poor, and the physically and mentally ill. Through these campaigns women were able to have at least some say in public affairs. They fought against slavery, flogging, and public executions. They lobbied for the reform of school prisons, poor laws, and child labor laws. With changing attitudes toward the natural world, animals — those abandoned or beaten by their owners — could now be included in this group of vulnerables. People who were cruel to animals, the reformers believed, lacked compassion and needed to be educated.

Children were the most obvious targets for moral reform. Nursery rhymes focusing on animals were used to teach children compassion. "Mary Had a Little Lamb," for instance, taught the reciprocal nature of love.

> *"What makes the lamb love Mary so?"*
> *The eager children cry —*
> *"Oh, Mary loves the lamb, you know,"*
> *The teacher did reply.*[8]

Children from working-class families were particularly singled out for reform. Working-class sports, such as cockfighting and bullbaiting, were associated with rabbles of drinking, gambling laborers who threatened the orderly world that the middle classes were trying to create. It is not surprising that these were among the first types of cruelty that animal protectionists outlawed. The Royal Society for the Prevention of Cruelty to Animals recommended in an annual report that the working classes, particularly their children, must: "be drilled and disciplined to virtue; to practice the duties if not to feel the sentiments of mercy and compassion." Consequently, the poor "will be brought up with their spirits more humbled, and will more fully fulfill their duties with . . . their fellow men."[9]

The increasing power of medical scientists threatened women's compassionate campaign. The new authority of science gave physicians a greater power to define morality. They appeared to connive with the law to keep women off the streets and in their homes. Under the new Contagious Diseases Acts, for instance, they carried out the medical examinations for venereal disease required of suspected prostitutes. Physicians now seemed to be challenging women's moral characters. Why, the women asked, weren't men being tested?[10]

Those against animal experiments—the so-called anti-vivisectionists—pointed to animal research to show how family physicians were turning into cool, calculating scientists who inflicted pain on the defenseless. One antivivisectionist publication laments that vivisection "makes brutes of those who should be kind and humane in the practice of the healing art."[11] Frances Power Cobbe, founder of the first antivivisection society, warned that "the cold rational materialism of science" was threatening "to freeze human emotion and sensibility." Antivivisection, she argued, "shielded the heart, the human spirit, from degradation at the hands of heartless science."[12]

The women were joined by church leaders and aristocrats, who also felt challenged by the rising authority of medical science. In 1822, "Humanity Dick" Martin successfully introduced into Parliament the first anti-cruelty bill—the Martin's Act. It was now an offense to beat horses or cattle. In 1824, philanthropists and religious leaders founded the first humane organization in England, the Society for the Prevention of Cruelty to Animals (SPCA; later to become "Royal"). By the middle of the nineteenth century, the society had initiated bills in Parliament against bullbaiting, cockfighting, and cruelty to dogs. Henry Bergh, the son of a wealthy New York shipbuilder, formed similar humane organizations in the United States, after being moved by peasants beating their horses on his travels in Russia.

Animal Protection and Domesticity in the 1950s

Widespread sentimentality over animals and increased interest in animal protection coincided with renewed attention to domestic life after the Second World War.[13] Women, now accustomed to a life of independence and camaraderie from working in factories, were pressured to surrender their jobs to men returning from the army. In Britain and the United States experts such as Dr. Spock and Freudian psychologists encouraged women to return to the home to recapture their femininity and to have more babies. The sociologist Talcott Parsons romanticized the family as a private subsystem. The ideal home, he said, would function through the "instrumental" work of men in the public world and the "expressive" labors of women at home. Whole industries grew up around domestic appliances, home furnishings, and family entertainments.[14] Women were once again to provide a haven of intimacy and emotional support for their children and husbands.

Pets became part of the image of picture-perfect nuclear families cared for by full-time mothers in detached suburban houses.[15] As in the Victorian humane movement, mothers once again taught children about compassion and morality through the plight of animals. Children of this generation still remember going with their mothers to see the Walt Disney movie *Bambi* and suffering with the young deer when he loses his mother to a hunter's bullet. Against this backdrop, several new animal protection groups formed in the United States, including the Humane Society of the United States and Friends of Animals. These were concerned not only with cats and dogs but also with wildlife, animals in entertainment, and slaughterhouse conditions.

In the mid-sixties, animal research again became an issue when the Humane Society of the United States joined

the Maryland State Police in a raid on the facilities of a
dog dealer who had been rounding up stray dogs to sell
to research laboratories. Captioned as a "Concentration
Camp for Dogs," a picture of the facilities made the front
pages of *Life* magazine.[16] The article alerted the public to
an "animal slave trade" in which ominous trucks appeared
in neighborhoods, rounding up unattended animals for
research.

The Recent Animal Rights Movement
and Women's Morality

In the late 1970s and early 1980s, animal protection
took on an altogether different mood. It was led by a new
wave of groups in the United States, including People for
the Ethical Treatment of Animals (PETA), In Defense of
Animals, Trans-Species Unlimited, and the underground
British group the Animal Liberation Front (ALF).

Henry Spira, Alex Pacheco, Ingrid Newkirk, and others
who founded these groups came from the humane societies and the environmental movement of the 1970s.[17] But
they were also critical of them. They were heavily influenced by the philosopher Peter Singer's book *Animal Liberation*. Singer curtly denies being an "animal lover" like Mrs.
Scott, a friend he describes who runs a pet hospital but
served him delicately cut ham sandwiches while discussing
her affection for pets. Singer aligns animal protection with
black and gay liberation. "This book makes no sentimental
appeals for sympathy towards 'cute' animals,"[18] he warns
his readers in his opening pages. When it comes to moral
considerations, Singer finds it no longer acceptable to dis-

criminate between pigs and dogs any more than between blacks and whites. This small paperback book, which I received automatically when I paid my subscription to PETA, soon turns to talk of "anger" and "outrage" over animal cruelty. The new "animal rights" activists influenced by it captured these emotions in well-publicized protests against biomedical research.

In 1975, for instance, Henry Spira spoke out against a series of experiments at the Museum of Natural History in New York City. The researchers were studying sexuality by cutting nerves in cats' penises, removing parts of their brains, and numbing their senses of smell. There was talk in the newspapers of taxpayers' money being wasted and cats being tortured. Even New York mayor Ed Koch took up the cause. It was enough for the National Institutes of Health (NIH) to withdraw their funding.

In 1981, Alex Pacheco, a young PETA member, got himself hired in the primate laboratories at the Institute for Behavioral Research in Silver Spring, Maryland. Pacheco found himself working for Edward Taub, a scientist who was studying limb damage in macaque monkeys. While Taub was out of the way, Pacheco documented and photographed monkeys driven delirious in the confines of small cages, wallowing in excrement, and suffering unbandaged wounds. On the evidence Pacheco supplied, police confiscated the monkeys and charged Taub with animal cruelty. After two appeals, the courts dropped the charges. As publicly funded laboratory subjects, the monkeys could not be protected under the state's existing anti-cruelty laws.[19] But the released monkeys became national celebrities as PETA and the NIH haggled over their possession.

In 1984, the Animal Liberation Front stole a set of video tapes from the head-trauma laboratory of the University of Pennsylvania Medical School. Known in the animal liberation world as the "Watergate tapes of the Animal Rights Movement,"[20] they reveal monkeys having their heads pounded by a steel plate in what looks like a diabolical machine. The surviving monkeys stagger around as if in a drunken stupor before the jeering technicians. NBC and Cable Network News flashed excerpts of the film on their nightly shows. The Department of Health and Human Services ordered the funding stopped. The following years witnessed further laboratory break-ins, thefts, accusations of animal cruelty, and fines and suspensions against medical centers and universities around the country.

By the end of the 1980s, according to a recent estimate, there were several hundred animal rights groups in the United States, and several thousand of the more moderate animal welfare organizations, such as local humane societies. One in five Americans claims to have donated money to animal protection organizations. In *The Animal Rights Crusade,* James Jasper and Dorothy Nelkin estimate that between five hundred thousand and one million of them donate to animal rights organizations.[21] In one of their most recent newsletters, PETA reports having five hundred thousand members in their organization alone.[22]

Animal rights organizations are diverse. PETA, for example, deals with a variety of animal rights causes. Others focus on single issues, such as animals in biomedical research (the New England Antivivisection Society) or factory farming (the Humane Farming Association). Some animal rights organizations boast professional membership (Psychologists for the Ethical Treatment of Animals, Physicians' Committee for Responsible Medicine), while others define their membership by specific liberationist causes (Feminists for Animal Rights, Gays and Lesbians for Animal Rights). Then there are organizations that define themselves by their tactics, such as fighting legislation (National Alliance for Animal Legislation, Animal Legal Defense Fund) or promoting awareness of animals through art, religion, and culture (Culture and Animals Foundation).[23]

Like the nineteenth-century animal protection movements, the recent animal rights movement in the United States has been described as a protest against professional science and modern industrial lifestyles. The animal rights activists in California, according to anthropologist Susan Sperling, are protesting the way nature has become besieged by technology.[24] Vivisection, she argues, is symbolic of how modern medicine, through measures such as vaccinations, pollutes the body. This account meshes with popular images of animal rights activists being anti-Enlightenment or anti-science.[25]

Animal rights activists, according to Jasper and Nelkin, are criticizing not just science but more broadly the selfish, profit-seeking behavior found in modern bureaucratic organizations. They believe that people should curb their individual behaviors so they do not harm others. They advocate, for example, preventive medicine, vegetarianism, and cruelty-free products over using animals for human ends. The authors interpret this as a criticism of "instrumentalism" — a utilitarian morality that pays attention only to the ends and not to the means of decisions.[26] The anti-instrumentalism common among animal rights activists, according to the authors, came from environmentalists, feminists, anti-nuclear and peace activists, and other 1960s protesters with whom animal rights activists share other beliefs, if not members.

As with the nurturing tradition of the nineteenth-century animal protectionists, modern feminists have claimed these criticisms of "cost-benefit" thinking for themselves. Psychologist Carol Gilligan, for example, believes that women find solutions to moral conflicts by attempting to preserve good relationships: Will people still talk to each other after the conflict? Can there be solutions in which no one gets hurt?[27] This ethic of "responsibility and care" is different from how men think, according to Gilligan. Men prefer to rely on laws, calculations, or universal principles to resolve moral dilemmas. They talk more of individual rights than responsibility and care. Women are brought up to cooperate, men to compete.

Some feminists — the "ecofeminists" — blame animal cruelty on the male psychology of competitiveness, individualism, and hierarchy. If women's values were to prevail, they argue, people would be kinder to animals and more tolerant of blacks, women, and gays. Rosemary Radford Ruether insists that it is in men's psychological makeup (the "masculine ego consciousness") to want to free themselves from femininity and nature, and to control them. This trait has led to ecological catastrophe and the oppression of women. Similarly, Estella Lauter believes that women are more respectful of nature than men are. In a study of women's art and literature, she found that "surprising numbers of women" have a "high degree of identification with nature." In women's art, the earth is seen not as "dead matter to be plundered, but wounded matter from which renewal flows. The two bodies, women's and earth's, are sympathetic." Feminists contrast women's sensitivity toward nature with the attitudes that prevail in the male-dominated worlds of science and business. In *The Death of Nature*, Carolyn Merchant bemoans the fact that by viewing the world "mechanistically" — as a machine rather than a living organism — science has "sanctioned the domination of both nature and women." And Sara Ruddick urges us to reject such manipulation and control over nature and adopt a "maternal" way of knowing, "governed by the priority of keeping, rather than acquiring, of conserving the fragile, of maintaining whatever is at hand and necessary to the child's life."[28] Meanwhile, in the world of international trade, Carol Adams draws parallels between the "traffic in women" and the "traffic in animals." Animals' and women's bodies are often seen as "disposable" or "usable" objects, produced and consumed in industry. Just as the feminists debunked the view that it is natural for women to serve men, we all need to disabuse ourselves, according to Adams, of the view that eating meat is natural and that humans are superior to animals.[29]

But special interest groups are not the only ones that have cornered the market on responsibility and care in advanced capitalist societies. In the past twenty years, scientists, politicians, business leaders, and members of the clergy have begun to develop their own styles of humanistic thinking. Many professional schools require their students to take classes in ethics. Politicians have been promoting the concept of "a kinder, gentler nation." Industries pronounce their concern for the environment.[30] Ethics have become big business. Animal protection is not just a movement against science. It is a movement within it.

The Beginnings of the Humane Movement in Science

Early animal experimenters shared the view that animals have no souls or power to reason and can therefore be treated like objects. But this did not stop them from feeling revulsion over animal experiments. One of the earliest animal experimenters, the Greek physician Claudius Galenus, refused to dissect the genitals of live animals or even dead ones in upright, humanlike positions. Also, he recommended that scientists use pigs or goats when dissecting the brain, to "avoid seeing the unpleasing expression of the ape when it is being vivisected."[31] Similarly, vivisectionists in the Renaissance period were not oblivious to animal suffering, but their curiosity often overshadowed their compassion for animals. The anatomist Realdo Colombo, for example, refers to "the poor dog" or "the unhappy dog" he is vivisecting but adds: "or rather the happy dog, because he affords to us a sight suitable for acquiring knowledge of the most beautiful things."[32] Even high-ranking clergymen "took great delight in attending his public vivisections," where he once demonstrated maternal love by injuring a newborn puppy in front of its mother.[33]

Throughout the seventeenth and early eighteenth centuries, animal research on the lymphatic system, blood circulation, and respiration persuaded medical scientists that animal research was the best way to learn about the human body. Experimenters overcame their squeamishness over animal cries by accepting Descartes' philosophy that animals are "beast machines" with no souls. According to one account, vivisectionists "beat their dogs with the utmost indifference and laughed at people who still maintained that animals could feel pain. The cries of dogs were interpreted as the mere creaking of the animal clockwork. They nailed the poor animals to boards by the four paws to dissect them while still alive, in order to watch the circulation of the blood, which was a subject of great discussion."[34]

By the middle of the eighteenth century, however, enthusiasm over such experiments became increasingly tainted with modern feelings toward animals. The reactions to Robert Boyle's infamous respiration experiments — in which he suffocated animals in a glass jar with an air pump — caught the imagination of the artist Joseph Wright. In *The Picture of the Air Pump*, Wright depicted an audience filled with curiosity, excitement, and fear at the ghastly spectacle, with women shielding their eyes in grief.

In 1824, the French physiologist François Magendie shocked his British counterparts with his physiology lectures in London. "Certain lecturers," the *London Medical Gazette* reported, "were represented in the most odious light as unnecessarily torturing and sacrificing the lives of rabbits, cats and dogs. The appalling experiments of Magendie were the topic of the day."[35] Yet by the end of the nineteenth century, even British physicians had widely adopted the continental practice of vivisection.[36]

How did British medical scientists overcome their repugnance toward animal research? In the first place, better anesthetics were now available. Another incentive was that vivisection looked more scientific than the old methods of clinical observations and case studies. Leaders of the newly emerging profession viewed vivisection as a rigorous and demanding intellectual activity that could be acquired only by special training and knowledge. This was important at a time when the aristocracy, judiciary, and clergy were all challenging the authority of medical scientists. As one commentator notes, "Medicine nailed its colours firmly to the mast of science"[37] in order to establish authority.

The medical community could sell itself on claims about the success of experimental medicine in developing therapies: an antitoxin for diphtheria, a treatment for diabetes, and control of tuberculosis. At the International Medical Congress in August 1881, the medical establishment resolved that animal experiments were justified and necessary to advance medicine. The following year, the presidents of the Royal College of Physicians and Surgeons established the Association for the Advancement of Medical Research to promote animal experimentation for learning about the human body, disease, remedies, inoculations, and poisons. In the United States, following antivivisectionist accusations of cruelty to animals at the newly opened Rockefeller Institute for Medical Research, the American Medical Association established a similar organization, the Council for the Defense of Medical Research, in 1907. By 1914, the vice president of the RSPCA and the president of the Boston Animal Protection League were actually praising biomedical researchers. The antivivisection movement was losing its widespread public support.[38]

But even then, undercurrents of antivivisectionism remained in the United States; at least they did in the minds of the editors at the *Journal of Experimental Medicine*, who developed euphemisms to protect themselves from accusations of cruelty. They substituted the word *animal* for *dog* to appease pet-lovers, and *fasting* for *starving, hemorrhaging* for *bleeding*, and *intoxicant* for *poison* in their publications. In one offending article on blood pressure in cats, an editor thought it prudent to replace "the brain was sliced off at various levels" with "the brain was removed." But defense against antivivisectionism was more than semantic. In 1946, the National Society for Medical Research introduced its prestigious "Dog Hero Award" to the survivors of cancer and heart research, "the Canine equivalent of the Nobel Prize." Its winners — Duke, Bozo, and Flossey — appeared triumphant in the national newspapers sporting their special new leather collars as medals.[39]

Animals and the Development of Medical Ethics

As in the late nineteenth century, the 1960s was a time in which the public questioned the authority of medical science. Increasing health costs, the growth of specialists over family physicians, and a general mistrust in experts encouraged more government regulation in the medical establishment. Whistle-blowers from inside the profession encouraged this mistrust by exposing abuses to human rights in medical experiments. Medical ethics were debated both within the medical community and outside it.[40] Legislation followed.

In 1966, the surgeon general of the United States issued a set of guidelines for all research funded by the Public Health Service. Local review committees now had to approve all research on human subjects, and researchers had to seek written consent from them. Animals became part of this movement for medical ethics. In that same year, Congress passed the first legislation concerning the use of animals in research, the Laboratory Animal Welfare Act — later known as the Animal Welfare Act. Prompted by news reports of an animal dealer who stole a dog and took it across state lines to sell to a laboratory, legislators were more concerned with protecting cat and dog owners from having their pets stolen by such dealers than with preventing cruelty in the laboratory. The legislation, therefore, covered only cat-and-dog holding facilities and required that dealers be licensed and inspected by the U.S. Department of Agriculture.

In the 1970s, amendments to the Animal Welfare Act extended its regulations to cover more animals but still excluded rats, mice, birds, horses, and farm animals — the majority of animals used in research. The amendments included more regulations about the handling, care, and treatment of animals in research and experimentation. They also required that anesthetics and tranquilizers be used according to the directions of a veterinarian.[41] The most recent legislation followed accusations of animal cruelty by the new animal rights organizations of the 1980s. Researchers now have to take into account animal pain and distress in their research designs, avoid multiple surgery on animals, exercise laboratory dogs, and even attend to the psychological well-being of their primates. The legislation also requires that every publicly funded animal research institution have a review committee that includes a public representative and a veterinarian to guard against cruelty in the labs.

As with medical practice in general, however, the increasing regulation of animal research has by no means been limited to the law and interest groups. It has also come from within the research community itself. In 1963, before any of the federal statutes were on the books, the National Institutes of Health began subjecting all federally funded agencies to the voluntary regulations outlined in its "Guide for the Care and Use of Laboratory Animals." There is now a multitude of accreditations, guidelines, regulations, and handbooks on laboratory animal care.

More recently, scientists have raised questions about the ethical treatment of animals in prestigious biomedical research and general scientific journals such as *Science*, the *New England Journal of Medicine*, and the *Journal of the American Veterinary Medical Association*. In a content analysis of the major journals, social analysts Mary Phillips and Jeri Sechzer found that scientists now routinely discuss ethics, animal pain, and alternatives to animal experimentation — in contrast to the 1970s when scientists simply complained about the encroachment of legislation.[42]

Medical journals have also taken an interest in the social-psychological aspects of animal research. Arnold Arluke, a sociologist who studies the everyday lives of animal researchers, has written about "uneasiness" among laboratory technicians for scientific journals such as *Lab Animal*. These technicians, he reports, adopted some lab animals as pets, kept photographs of them, and even deified them as heroes and martyrs to science like the dog-hero prize win-

ners of an earlier generation.[43] Other scientists and naturalists, such as Jane Goodall and Dian Fossey (author of *Go-
rillas in the Mist*), have gone further than these technicians
by popularizing a caring, respecting attitude toward their
"subjects."[44]

And outside the world of science, on the edges of sociology, psychology, anthropology, and philosophy, there has
been a movement to write about animals not just as part of
society's "material subsistence," or as the pampered ac-
cessories of an aging aristocracy, but as the long unrecog-
nized, unacknowledged, and neglected sources of therapy,
culture, identity, religion, and morality.[45]

As our old justifications for exploiting animals have been
stripped away, we have found new ways of reconciling our
conscience over cruelty. The nineteenth-century feminists
included animals in their compassionate campaigns. Humane societies in the 1950s drew attention to pet theft and
promoted compassion for wildlife as animals came to sym-
bolize restored domestic life. The animal rights activists of
the 1970s and 1980s took their cues from the liberation
movements launched by blacks, women, and Hispanics.
The ecofeminists preached maternal responsibility and
care for animals. Biomedical scientists deified and mar-
tyred lab animals, while politicians, lawyers, and administrators regulated, legislated, and lobbied for their protection. These trends, as historian Keith Thomas points out,
have grown out of contradictory developments in our lifestyles: our sprawling cities, our desire to control "pests,"
our ever more efficient ways of slaughtering and processing meat, and our reliance upon animal-based science. We

have, to paraphrase the poet Oliver Goldsmith, come to "pity and eat the objects of our compassion."[46] What follows is a description of how two different groups in the College Town community experienced and attempted to resolve this paradox.

Three

The College Town

Picture a small college town in the southern United States. University life dominates the town, strung out with colonial-style buildings connected by red-brick paths laid across grassy verges. Bookstores, cafés, and restaurants line the main strip that runs south of the campus. On a typical Saturday afternoon in the fall, "a Footballing Saturday," the place is ablaze in the university's colors, and blond, golden-skinned students fill the sidewalks. The parking lots are closed, even to faculty, and become a playground for tailgate parties presided over by stocky middle-aged men in baseball caps.

At night on Jordan Street, which runs parallel to the main strip, music blasts from dilapidated fraternity houses, and fraternity boys in torn shorts that reach down to their knees sit on the window ledges overlooking the front lawns, bathed in the soft warm smell of fermented beer. In the morning, the street will be strewn with crushed beer cans and the trees draped in toilet paper of the university's colors.

The College Town and the surrounding cities boast one of the highest concentrations of Ph.D.'s in the United

States. Known for their liberalism, residents often quote a
prominent southern politician as wanting to build a fence
around the town to prevent its liberal causes from spilling
out. During my stay there, a political science graduate student, who always wore denims and a rat-tail haircut, chased
a CIA recruiting agent out of town with a bottle of tomato
ketchup as a protest against American interference across
its southern borders. Some students threatened to boycott
classes to protest the Gulf War. Others fought successfully
to establish a black cultural center. And every day, College
Town residents shopped at their local cooperatives and
filled their biodegradable bags with organic peanut butter
and radiation-free apples.

Yet the College Town gives a misleading picture of the
rest of the state, which has high rates of illiteracy and conservative values. I spent long holiday weekends in some of
the smaller towns near the mountains or on the coast with
the students I taught. Here, there were more churches
than gas stations and families spent their Saturdays in front
of the television watching car racing or the country music
channel, only to break the monotony by getting into one of
several sedans in the gravel driveway to bring back fast food
or cruise the shopping malls. My students' brothers, sisters,
and cousins casually told jokes about "niggers," and I recall one particularly still and humid summer afternoon, at
a street fair in Farmsboro, about an hour's drive from the
College Town, when a jeans-clad, bearded man in a baseball cap handed me a leaflet urging me to join the Ku Klux
Klan. So although the College Town includes many supporters of liberal causes, some of its residents grew up in
rural settings and hold traditional attitudes.

In contrast, other residents had come to the College Town with more liberal backgrounds from the Midwest or West Coast to take post-graduate degrees or begin their professional careers. Ascending professional ranks, many wondered whether they had left the counter-culture far behind them.

But the College Town is a gentle place. Residents enjoy restaurants and hotels that are familylike or "folksy" — as I often heard them described. The same sense of familiarism extends to the most fleeting encounters. One says "Hey" in a soft voice when meeting a stranger coming home late at night on the bike path leading back from the campus, where townhouses turn to mill houses with porches and rocking chairs. This code of gentility extends to political affairs. Like the pro- and anti-abortion activists that sociologist Fay Ginsburg studied in a small town in the Midwest,[1] even the most ardent opponents in the animal rights controversy address one another in a code of civility and politeness. To be too aggressive, too noisy, only creates more problems. The dean of a medical school near the College Town once explained to me, "There's an old Southern proverb: 'You should never raise more snakes than you can conveniently kill.' And sometimes, if you publicize a topic too much, you can create more problems than you started with."

Not only is the College Town home to one of the oldest state universities in the country and a prestigious medical school, but it is located near a research park with corporate and government research institutes, three other medical schools, and a veterinary college. Many College Town residents look at technology and large-scale corporate business with a critical eye. They lament the rapid development that the university and other industries have brought to the area: thick concrete belts of highways and multifaceted glass-faced corporate headquarters with artificial lakes splattered over the landscape in a postmodern sprawl. Yet their lives are also embedded in these developments. Many work at the university, its medical school, or the research park as students, teachers, administrators, and clerks. This is the story of a group of such people who were involved in either protesting or defending animal research.

Animals Anon

The Lunatic Years

Animal rights activism in the state emerged out of and in opposition to a humane movement that began in the 1970s. It did so with the help of discontented individuals, legal experts, highly publicized protests, and the growing national animal rights movements of the 1980s. Animal protectionists in the 1970s were preoccupied with conditions at the county-run animal pounds, where abandoned animals were killed, according to one activist, with carbon monoxide off the back of a pickup truck. In some instances, these protests resulted in the humane societies taking over the pounds. At least one county responded by setting up a shelter advisory board of concerned citizens to monitor them. These early animal protectionists were not initially concerned with animal research.

An influential figure in the humane movement was a woman whom I call Betty, an English professor at a university in the state's capital, who founded Animals Anon. "I can be a real bitch," Betty once warned me. And I could believe her. A prickly, middle-aged woman, she was later to be ousted by the organization she founded. Her possessiveness of it, and specifically her worry about its public image, would not allow her to delegate authority. Activists accused her of being dictatorial. The name Animals Anon, although fictitious, reflects Betty's perception that she and her supporters were, in the eyes of lawmakers, "the lunatic fringe."

Like many of the early animal rights activists I met, Betty volunteered time raising money for her local humane society. She rose quickly through the ranks of the organization and became a board member. But she was constantly dissatisfied. "All I ever heard about," she told me, "was how can we make more money." The humane society did improve life at the shelter for abandoned animals, but Betty saw no point in helping them five days before they were killed and dumped in the city landfill. It would have been better, she thought, to spend the money on encouraging people to spay, neuter, and adopt animals. She felt helpless not knowing what to do. That sense of helplessness is a theme common to other animal rights activists' recruitment stories.

Betty started Animals Anon in 1982 to deal with this issue of abandoned animals. Until then, local animal shelters could sell their unclaimed animals for a small profit to biomedical researchers for experimentation. Betty's husband, an attorney, pointed out to Betty that the laws that permitted pounds to sell their animals to researchers were ambiguously written. Public health officials were exploiting this ambiguity to argue that the sales were perfectly legal. Betty wanted to introduce a bill — the Pet Protection Bill —

to change the language of the law in such a way that selling abandoned pets to research would violate anti-cruelty statutes. But the humane society refused to support her, arguing that researchers would resort to bringing animals from other states, thus inflicting more misery on them.

Betty initiated a public hearing. The morning after, she burrowed through the local newspaper to find the story. It had not occurred to her that the incident was considered important enough to make the front page rather than the human interest sections toward the back where the newspapers usually aired animal stories. The Pet Protection Bill failed to convince legislators that it is inhumane to sell pound animals to research. But the publicized hearing did provoke a rash of letters to the editor supporting Betty's proposal. This was an opportunity for her to break away from the reluctant humane society and form her own animal protection group. She contacted her supporters and organized them into three chapters of a new statewide organization, Animals Anon.

In the four years that followed, Betty continued to rely on public events and media coverage to attract more supporters. On April 19, 1986, nationally known animal rights activists, including Tom Regan, Cleveland Amory, Neal Bernard, and the former animal researcher Donald Barnes, gave speeches at the state capital. This time the protest was over a different issue. The army at Fort Lingham, a military base out on the coast, had been shooting goats to train surgeons how to stitch up war wounds. Booths, banners, and information tables sprouted up around the capital buildings, where protesters made speeches and children twirled around in the sunshine on the lawns. Organizers urged participants to set up their own animal rights groups. Animals Anon added five more chapters to its existing three.

Animals Anon was also involved with other animal causes. Betty spoke out against trapping at local wildlife groups. She challenged universities to abandon the use of animals for teaching. Other members organized protests against the slaughter of seals in Canada, found homes for displaced wild burros, and held regular anti-fur campaigns at shopping malls. They gave public lectures, staffed information tables, distributed animal rights literature to public libraries, and talked to high schools about vegetarianism. Again, they relied on the literature and information from the national animal rights organizations such as People for the Ethical Treatment of Animals (PETA), Trans-Species Unlimited, and the Fund for Animals, which were already gaining notoriety.

The mid-1980s, according to one of the organization's chroniclers, was a time in which Animals Anon was beginning to be taken seriously. At least one local retailing chain closed its fur salon. Penalties for dog fighting were doubled. Animal researchers were now agreeing to meet with activists, and Animals Anon members were invited to represent the animal rights position on local television and radio debates about animal research. Chapter coordinators interpreted these events as major victories in what had seemed impossible battles.

The Rosenthal Years

In the second half of the 1980s, Animals Anon continued to be involved with a variety of animal rights issues: protests against circuses and rodeos, deer hunting competitions, and animal dissections in high school biology classes. Members marched alongside those of other respectable charitable organizations in the state's Christmas parade. They organized vegetarian meals and staffed information booths at shopping malls and state fairs. They raised money by organizing dog washes and animal festivals and sponsoring bowling tournaments and rock band nights. One supporter even loaned out his hair salon to raise money for the organization.

As volunteers with limited time and resources, however, the activists preferred to concentrate their efforts on a small number of campaigns—campaigns in which much effort had already been spent and in which victory seemed imminent. College Town activists focused on two. The first had been started in 1989 by two activists who became suspicious about animal cruelty at one of the university's animal holding facilities deep in the countryside, several miles outside the College Town. The activists ominously called it "the Farm." They alerted PETA, whose investigators pushed their way past animal caretakers and entered the facility with cameras. Soon after, photographs of mangy cats and dogs with diarrhea, along with a report on the solitary life of a monkey in a cage at the Farm, appeared in PETA's newsletter.

A few years earlier, close to "World Day for Laboratory Animals"—when animal rights groups all over the country protest animal experimentation—Douglas, the coordinator of the College Town chapter, had urged a young graduate student, Saul, to start a student animal rights group at the College Town university. Douglas wanted to have a protest on the campus but could do so only if it was organized by a student group. Saul had just moved to the College Town from Boston, where he had read some of the most graphic animal rights books around. He was, in his own words, "ripe" for action. When the news of the Farm raid broke, Saul was angered that university officials refused to disclose details about their research. He proposed that the university create a clearing house to find alternatives to using animals in their research and teaching. University officials granted him a tour of the animal holding facilities but denied him access to research proposals and the meetings where a university committee reviewed them. Feeling shut out of decisions about animal research, a group of students eventually filed a law suit against the university to get hold of the proposals, along with minutes of the committee's meetings. At the height of the campaign, Saul organized a silent vigil outside the chancellor's house and PETA placed an advertisement in the university's *Daily Phoenix*, offering a two-hundred-dollar reward for evidence of animal cruelty at the College Town university.

The students had allies. A lawyer member of Animals Anon agreed to take on the case but resigned after researchers defeated him in the first hearing. The activists then turned to a lawyer from one of the national organizations who specialized in animal rights issues and had won similar cases for other groups. PETA representatives also came to the College Town. In a seminar called "Animal Rights 101," they publicized details of animal experiments at the College Town university that they culled from the abstracts of electronic data bases in the library.

The second campaign began in 1985, before the Farm raid, in a larger city about ninety minutes' drive from the

College Town. Several years after Betty's Pet Protection Bill, stories were continuing to break about pets winding up in laboratories. Seth, the organization's vice president, received a desperate call from a cat owner who believed that her cat had been stolen by animal dealers for research. He traced this woman's cat to animal laboratories at a local university and rescued the animal, apparently, "in the nick of time."

Animal protectionists in the Larger City turned their attention from conditions at their local pound to its policy of selling unwanted animals to biomedical research. Animal rights activists began to pressure the Shelter Advisory Board to stop selling animals to the Larger City's university, and small groups of protesters holding candles started to assemble regularly outside the pound. It was at one of the advisory board hearings that the activists first met Rachel Rosenthal.[2]

The ambitious daughter of a Jewish immigrant, Rosenthal was a young biologist who had just moved to the Larger City university. She had not been there long when she began using cats from the shelter for neurological research on the spinal cord. Rosenthal accepted an invitation from the Shelter Advisory Board to come to the pound one night and defend using pound animals for research. After inspecting Rosenthal's labs, the board voted to continue to allow her to use the pound cats. According to Rosenthal, the advisory board announced the vote in a room with three hundred animal rights activists where you could, she recalls, hear a murmur among them as the decision came in. Infuriated by the result, they went to the university's library and to Rosenthal herself hungry for details on what was happening to cats in her labs.

Admittedly, the direct applications of Rosenthal's work are not easy to understand. Much of it involves painstaking measurements and a knowledge of neurological and chemical processes. Neurologists have written much about how injuries to the spine disrupt the delicate balance of chemicals that allow cells to function in the gray matter of the spinal cord. When the spine is injured, the cells swell with large amounts of sodium and calcium, damaging tissues that conduct nerve impulses. Over time, the balance of chemicals is restored. Rosenthal used cats to study this process because their nervous systems are similar to those of humans. In particular, she was interested in whether certain chemical blockers could help bring these cells back to recovery in a short time. Official university information sheets on the project did not say how she was going to do this, but Animals Anon literature includes pictures of cats clamped in a stereotaxic device, with electrodes and tubes trailing from their limbs, and describes how Rosenthal crushed their spinal cords.

A small, sullen woman I call Dee led the campaign against Rosenthal. After giving up her job as a social worker, Dee sought out Animals Anon while looking for volunteer work in the newspapers. She learned about Rosenthal's experiments at the first meeting she attended. In disbelief, she met with both Rosenthal and a university administrator at the Larger City, David Nathan, to learn more about the cat experiments.

Dee and her supporters began to distribute literature

about cats' being paralyzed in Rosenthal's labs to the university chancellor, alumni, animal rights and welfare organizations, and even to cat fancier magazines. So successful was the publicity, that the issue aired on a nationally syndicated radio show hosted by Paul Harvey, apparently winning his support. Animal rights activists, sometimes over a hundred of them, congregated with placards outside the university's science buildings on the annual World Day for Laboratory Animals. They did so from 1988 to 1991.

By the time I attended my first animal rights meeting on February 20, 1989, Animals Anon had fifteen hundred dues-paying members and eleven chapters. Its members had also encouraged students to organize groups on their campuses. There were now animal rights activists all over the state that met regularly in church halls, recreation centers, and student unions.

Day to Day with the Animal Rights Activists

I imagined life in the animal rights movement to be a life lived on the edge — a secret underworld of clandestine encounters, dangerous missions, and lawless self-sacrifice. This image of the animal rights movement is one I had seen promoted in journalistic accounts. But there was another image that came to mind also. I grew up in England, where my mother had been marginally involved with figures in the dog-breeding world while buying pure-bred Shetland sheep dogs as pets. I recall one couple we visited who had made dogs their life. They had turned the living room of their semi-detached house into a giant whelping box that stank of urine. They talked about dog pedigrees and kennels with much the same seriousness that parents might talk about which college to send their children to. I imagined a meeting of animal rights activists to be an emotional kind of self-help group for pet owners who, unable to cope, have given up on the world of people.

But a monthly organizational meeting in Animals Anon is, by activists' own accounts, businesslike. The meetings take place in the institutionalized pastel environment of church halls and recreation centers, above the relentless throbbing of aerobics classes or the spiritual murmuring of self-help groups. Animal rights meetings are formal and sober events. Some activists do not welcome small-talk and socializing. Most do not consider their fellow activists to be among their close friends. They arrive at meetings after work, flushed from running, and clutching notepads and newspaper clippings of animal rights events and letters to the editor. After a mechanical introduction of new members, activists get down to reviewing the month's activities and planning upcoming events: protests to be attended, information tables to be staffed, leaflets to be handed out, and letters to be written. The locus of action is the sign-up sheet, passed from member to member, on which you are supposed to put down your name to organize or help out in an activity.

In my early meetings, I was impressed by the precision with which activists plan events. Do you need a permit at a protest? What happens if you are arrested? Will you lose your job if you protest an institution where you work? When protesting a research institute, you wear a suit and "look spiffy." At the circus you don't protest, you just give out information. At the rodeo you don't talk to anyone, you just hold your sign. Animal rights activists go to the library to learn about the research going on in their local universities. Animal cruelty has to be documented with minute precision. There is a multitude of laws and organizations that deal with animal cruelty. These have to be researched and understood before you can do anything.

To be sure, activists joke about planting bombs. But among those I spent time with, joke about it is all they ever did. Betty considered even civil disobedience "a very serious matter." Joking about being terrorists was how the activists distanced themselves from that label. Although James Jasper and Dorothy Nelkin in *The Animals Rights Crusade* interpret an "I'm an Animal Rights Terrorist" badge as a confession that many activists actually embrace this identity,[3] Animals Anon participants used such slogans only to express their cynicism toward it. At one meeting, activists laughed hard at a story in the *Daily Phoenix* about clerks at the College Town university opening their mail in the parking lots for fear that they will be blown up, or about Rosenthal building security systems to protect herself from a terrorist attack. For several weeks, there was a running joke about FBI agents scouting around in sunglasses and carrying hand-held radios at protests.

Paradoxically, animal rights activists often support organizations that are notorious for animal rights terrorism, such as the Animal Liberation Front (ALF). In fact, many activists I met wanted to be part of this organization and did not consider what ALF does to be terrorist. How they rationalized their support is a topic I take up in Chapter Six when I talk about radicals in the movement.

There are few formal positions, titles, or roles in Animals Anon. Saul believes that all members should take part in decision making, but this rarely happened. Until 1992, Betty headed the entire organization with Seth, whom I never met. All decisions had to go through her. I felt her presence at meetings even though she was not there. The only other formal position was that of chapter coordinator. In the College Town and Larger City chapters, the meetings were dominated by a few charismatic men, and one of them was not even a coordinator. A group of three to six core activists did most of the planning by telephone before the meetings. It was a symbolic democracy.

How does someone get involved with the animal rights movement? It is misleading to think that one "joins" the animal rights movement in the way that one joins, say, the American Automobile Association or the Rotary Club. One can feel part of the movement without ever attending a meeting. For instance, a college student announced at her first Animals Anon meeting, "I feel like I'm involved with it, but I've never attended a group." She was referring to her vegetarianism and the hours she had spent reading animal rights literature. There were some activists I heard about but never saw at the meetings. They researched animal cruelty and wrote letters from home. As Saul put it, you learn most about animal rights "on the couch."

In fact, for most activists, awareness of animal suffering begins many years before knowing about the animal rights movement. All twenty of the activists I interviewed began the story of their journey into the movement by saying that they had "always loved animals." They grew up with pets. "I could never understand why kids would throw rocks at cats, or do the little pranks that kids do," one man told me. Most of them kept many pets and considered them part of the family. Two men spoke of their love or fascination for wild-life and nature, although this did not preclude them from killing animals. They hunted as a way to be close to nature.

Most activists admitted having had vague or uneasy feelings about animal suffering before becoming involved in Animals Anon. They had seen animals on their way to slaughter or witnessed an animal struggling in a hunt or prepared an animal carcass for a meal. At the time, however, they tried to put these experiences out of their minds. A few years before Dee became involved with the animal rights movement, for instance, she was having lunch with a friend at the local grill. A woman walked into the restaurant wearing a fur coat. Aware that wearing fur was cruel, Dee turned to her friend and whispered, "That fur coat looked better on its original owner."

"You're no different than she is," her friend replied, loudly.

"What are you talking about? I don't own any fur," Dee argued.

"How do you think that chicken got on your plate?"

"I knew as soon as he said that, that he was right," Dee recalls, "but I put it out of my mind because I didn't want to deal with it. I couldn't deal with how that chicken got on my plate." Often it is those who do not share the activists' feelings who reinforce them. The more activists criticize others for animal cruelty, the more they are forced to confront their own role in it.

For most activists, affection for animals translated into volunteer work at the local humane societies. Two women came to the shelter to adopt pets and never left. Others came, like good Samaritans, with bundled-up animals they had found injured on the road. They came with blankets and with time on their hands to play with the kittens, walk the dogs, and even rise to the ranks of educators, cruelty investigators, and adoption officers. But rather than relieving them of their guilt over animal suffering, the shelters could also reinforce this feeling. It was here that some of the fledgling animal rights activists learned about unwanted animals ending up in parking lots and dumpsters and then finally being sold by pounds to research labs. They sought out animal rights organizations and literature that supported their opposition to the pounds' policies.

Four of the twenty activists that I interviewed came to Animals Anon from the shelters. Six sought out Animals Anon after receiving literature about cruelty to animals from the national animal rights organizations such as PETA, the Fund for Animals, and Friends for Life. Another six came after seeing Animals Anon's literature distributed at the local grocery cooperative, vegetarian groups, mall tables, information booths, or protests. Three activists learned of the organization through the group's advertisements or protests covered in their local newspapers and on television news shows. One woman heard about it through her college roommate's sister, who asked her to write a letter of protest against Rosenthal.

What kinds of people are in the animal rights movement? It is difficult to characterize the animal rights activists as a distinctive socioeconomic group. The twenty activists that I interviewed ranged in age from twenty-five to sixty-three. Three were over fifty. Seven were in their early to mid-forties, while another two were in their late thirties. The rest were in their mid-twenties to early thirties. Animals Anon found it difficult to attract undergraduates to the movement. Campus animal rights activism was short-lived and faded as soon as the examination schedule began and the semester ended. I only once saw teenagers at a meeting.

Sixteen of the twenty animal rights activists I interviewed were women, a reflection of the overall predominance of women in the organization. In the College Town, on average, almost 70 percent of those who attended the monthly organizational meetings were women. This figure was 80 percent in the Larger City. Eight of those I interviewed were single. Two were divorced. The rest were married. Only two of the activists had children.

Four of the activists were professionals. There was a college professor, an attorney, a social worker, and a preschool teacher. Another three were undergoing or about to undergo professional training in graduate school. Most of the others were in high-status, white-collar administrative positions (a city supervisor, a social worker, and a finance manager) or in skilled technical occupations (a computer programmer, a research technician, and a technical writer). One woman was a piano teacher. Another worked as an advocate for abused children. Four women were in semi- or unskilled occupations—a decorator, a waitress, a receptionist, and an office clerk. One was an undergraduate. Two of the activists worked part-time. Their occupations as well as their lifestyles bear out the common assumption that animal rights activists tend to be middle-class. I met them in smart offices or rambling houses in peaceful middle-class suburbs, where I recall one wintry dusk looking enviously out from my old gray car at their homes decked out with Christmas fripperies. But then again, I also met a few, usually those known as radicals, who lived in ramshackle trailers and dilapidated houses in the countryside. I recall meeting one poor woman, who was "kind of in between jobs," at a bar-and-grill restaurant just off the highway between the state capital and the College Town. Although there were plenty of vegetarian options on the menu, she ordered only bread and soup because she could not afford anything more and I, equally broke, felt ashamed that I could not pay for her.

Those I interviewed also bore out the accepted notion that animal rights activists hold the postmaterialist, romanticist, and liberationist views shared by the social movements of the 1960s.[4] All but two of the activists had been in organizations related to the women's movement (the National Organization of Women and rape crisis centers), the environmental movement (the Sierra Club, Greenpeace, the Nature Conservancy), or global issues (Amnesty International, the peace movement, Central America). But this was not unusual for College Town residents. And then again, one of the women I interviewed was a pro-life activist, and two described their backgrounds as conservative and traditional and said that they had never been in a protest movement before.

Yet as their occupations suggest, many of these people's lives were in some way involved with science, technology, and corporate life. In one survey, psychologist Harold Herzog found animal rights activists enrolled in biology graduate programs too.[5] In fact, it is sometimes through their technical and professional skills that activists become involved with the animal rights movement. One of those I interviewed first learned about animal suffering in medical experiments after reading abstracts of research in the hallways where she worked at a medical school. Another woman learned about Animals Anon through a friend she met on a vegetarian computer network.

Responses to Animals Anon

The Pro-Research Movement

According to Betty, scientists were on the scene defending the sale of pound animals for research when she first tried to introduce the Pet Protection Bill in 1982. Three years later, Rosenthal called research administrators and local physicians together again to help persuade the Shelter Advisory Board to release pound animals for experimentation. It was not until 1989, however, that David Nathan, the research administrator in the Larger City, called his counterparts from research institutions all over the state to form a local affiliate of the National Association for Biomedical Research (NABR).

Nathan trained as a physicist. He had spent fifteen years working for the National Science Foundation, where he funded and planned international research programs. Feeling burned out from traveling throughout the world, he settled in the Larger City, doing much the same kind of work but in the gentler surroundings of a grassy campus. Nathan had not been there long when he began to read angry letters to the editors of the local papers about Rosenthal's research. Occasionally, he would receive requests from activists for information about Rosenthal's work. The chancellor appointed Nathan to be Rosenthal's spokesperson. Soon Dee and her followers appeared at his office. By all accounts, these early meetings went along with their usual southern politeness. The animal rights activists appeared to Nathan to be willing to compromise by suggesting that Rosenthal breed her own cats rather than rely on those from the pound. In a letter to Nathan, however, Dee denied making this suggestion and demanded that the research be stopped completely. Nathan flew into a rage. These people wanted to stop all animal research, he thought.

It appeared to Nathan that the animal rights activists were dominating the press coverage. There was no one to speak for the university. He called administrators at other universities and institutes in the research park and quickly organized a local branch of the already established NABR. The association had been operating in other states, most actively in California. It employed a coterie of speakers and public relations officers to educate the public about animal research and counter the animal rights activists' claims about animal experimentation.

One Saturday afternoon in the winter of 1989, as sleet turned to snow, ninety people, representing forty-five institutions, came to Nathan's first meeting at a research institute in the park. Nathan formed a working group with fifteen of his supporters and hired a public relations specialist. She raised money by soliciting membership dues from the local medical schools, veterinary schools, universities, pharmaceutical firms, private research institutes, and patient groups, such as the American Diabetes Association. Later that year, two first-year science graduate students who were enraged by PETA's grim portrayal of the

Farm started a campuswide organization to counter the animal rights activists in the College Town. It too was part of a national pro-research organization, the Coalition for Animals and Animal Research. Faculty, administrators, graduate students, curious on-lookers from the campus animal rights group, and older people whom I had never seen before filled a large classroom. Graduate students formed a similar group at the Larger City university.

But Nathan had to consider one fact that the animal rights activists did not: "Professors don't like to go and preach on the street corner like evangelists and protest groups." Instead, NABR public events were slick, audio-visual-aided symposia and conferences held on university campuses. Nobel Prize scientists, surgeons, and patients came to testify in formal speeches on behalf of biomedical research.

At the same time, Nathan wanted the pro-research movement to look "grass-roots," to include not just anonymous scientists in obscure specialties but also the familiar faces of general practitioners, veterinarians, and high school teachers. So for a few summers, when I marched into town with a hundred and fifty or so animal rights activists who were protesting Rosenthal, a thin line of biomedical research supporters met us, sheepishly standing in a line at the curbside with identical posters of children saved by animal research. For a few tense moments, animal rights activists and research supporters stared across at one another.

To help win grass-roots support, Nathan turned to his public relations officer. A graduate in sociology, she worked out of a beige-colored prefabricated office suite in the state's capital and traveled around the region garnering subscriptions and giving workshops to researchers on how to counter animal rights activists in front of the media. Like Animals Anon, the organization produced its own share of brochures as well as literature handed down from its national counterparts. Pro-researchers tried to get these documents into high school classrooms and the clinics of local physicians and veterinarians.

The Institutional Animal Care and Use Committees

Aside from this public relations organization, there was another response to the animal rights movement. An amendment in the 1985 Animal Welfare Act required that every federally funded research institution have at least five people serve on an "Institutional Animal Care and Use Committee" (or, "IACUC," as it was more familiarly known). The committee was supposed to inspect all animal research proposals and animal holding facilities for violations of the complex web of regulations surrounding laboratory animal welfare.

I first met Dwayne Spalding, the committee chair in the College Town. A professor of pathology and the associate dean of the medical school, he was the highest-ranking member of the committee. There was also the immunologist Henry Weiss, several other younger researchers from the school of pharmacy, and the university's head veterinarian, George Cramer. The National Institutes of Health regulations required the university to have a member from outside the community also. Spalding found a retired nurse to fill this position — a matronly woman who lived in one of the enormous retirement complexes on the edge of town.

Every month in the College Town, the Larger City, and other biomedical research organizations in the state, the committee met in a conference room to review stacks of proposals submitted by research scientists to undertake animal experiments. Every six months they inspected the animal facilities. The committee in the College Town began their inspections in Cramer's office. From this brightly lit, cozy room they entered the underground world of the animal holding facilities — a maze of corridors painted in institutional glossy hues of brown and beige whose ceilings house long fluorescent lights, some with cracked coverings, buried among large black exhaust pipes, concertined like giant colons. With notepads in hand — checklists of problems to look for — the committee members peered into windowless rooms with incubators of warm, twitching rodents and larger wire cages of rabbits and chickens. And then they filed out into sunshine so brilliant after the dark facilities they had to squint and shield their eyes. The inspection tour continued with a ten-minute drive to the Farm. After PETA entered the facility, the university had installed a new security gate and Cramer would always forget the code number to open it. The place looks deserted from the outside. There are a few scruffy long white trailers where the overnight staff live. The facility itself is built from enormous white cinderblocks. The ceilings are low with the usual long fluorescent lights. Barking explodes so fiercely as people approach the Farm that the caretakers have to cover their ears with thick muffs. It was clearing out time when I joined the inspection. A young woman in a blue boiler suit and long green rubber boots was sweeping mounds of red claylike excrement with a long broom into the gutters at the side of the dog pens. But as I mentioned above, the animal facilities reminded me much of the animal shelters where many activists volunteered.

The IACUCs were drawn into the controversy when animal rights activists demanded to inspect the minutes of their meetings. They were drawn into the controversy in another way too. They came to represent the practical embodiment of the researchers' criteria for ethical research. It was the committees' role to ensure that useful, humane research occurred. Some committee members were also spokespersons for the pro-research organization.

Research Supporters and Animal Rights Activists

How are those who actively support animal research different from the animal rights activists? The twenty research supporters that I interviewed (including IACUC members) were, on average, ten years older than the animal rights activists. Eight were over fifty. Senior faculty were more likely than juniors to be appointed to the IACUC. After reading the ecofeminists, I expected there to be few women supporting animal research. But I found equal numbers of men and women at pro-research conferences and symposia. There were seven women among those I interviewed.

Ten research supporters I interviewed sat on IACUCs in the College Town, the Larger City, or at the institute in the park. They had research backgrounds in a variety of health or animal sciences. The other ten were involved in the

Association for Biomedical Research — in university administration, biomedical research, or public relations. Most of
these people had backgrounds in science, with the exception of the public relations specialist, a legal advisor, and an
administrator at the College Town university who had a
Ph.D. in religion. Fourteen of the twenty people I interviewed on the research side of the controversy had actually
done animal research.

How did these people become involved in the animal
research controversy? Most saw it as an extension of their
everyday work. As researchers, they had been targeted by
the animal rights activists and felt that they had to defend
themselves. Or as administrators, they had been charged
by their deans and chancellors to defend their institutions
or appointed to serve on the IACUC.

As with the animal rights activists, many of the animal research supporters described being aware of the controversy
long before Animals Anon or even the recent animal rights
movement. For those who actually did research, their involvement began at the moment they started doing animal
experiments, usually in the 1960s. "The debate interested
me," Cathy O'Brien, a psychologist in the College Town
told me. "I think I've been involved in these issues about
how animals are treated and the role animals play in our
lives virtually all my life." Her earliest experiments involved
humans. Prompted by newly established review boards for
human subjects, she recalled, "I had to think about what
I was doing to those subjects." Later, when she came to
animal research, she read Peter Singer's *Animal Liberation*.
For twelve years, she sat on a subcommittee of the American Psychological Association that discussed ethical issues

surrounding animal research. From her involvement in that committee, she thinks, her name appeared on a list of researchers targeted by a New York–based animal rights group. The list was passed on to Animals Anon, and she received threatening letters. A spokesperson in the university administration asked her to write a lay summary of her research in case the animal rights activists challenged the university about it. Knowing that she was interested in the controversy, graduate students in the campus pro-research group asked her to give a presentation on the animal rights movement at a pro-research conference in the College Town. Thus, as with the animal rights activists, initial concerns about animal welfare, combined with organizational recruitment and challenges to her use of animals, brought her into the controversy.

Indeed, all but a few researchers expressed, at least in private, a degree of identification with the animal rights activists' feelings of indebtedness toward animals, and guilt over using them for human ends. These feelings are not new among scientists, or among any of us. For most of the time they remain implicit or unacknowledged. But in the animal research controversy, they become problematic and have to be dealt with. What differentiates animal rights activists from supporters of animal research, I point out in the next two chapters, is not so much their affection for animals or their initial attitudes toward science and technology but the way they reconcile their feelings in the context of their everyday experiences with animal suffering, their work, and their organizations.

Four

All Our Sins

Environmentalists, civil rights campaigners, anti-nuclear protesters, and other special interest groups are often blamed for creating an over-regulated society. Since the Second World War, according to Peter Berger's *The Capitalist Revolution*, these groups represent a new class in Western democracies.[1] They value "quality of life" over money and objects. Living off government payrolls, they work to expand the government's role over private interests. Welfare organizations, environmental protection agencies, human rights commissions, and watch-dog groups, then, come to regulate everything from sexual conduct to smoking in public.

Animal welfare is more regulated than it has ever been, too. But this is not what compelled the activists I met to take part in the movement for animal rights. Activists saw their participation in the movement in much more personal terms. They sought personal empowerment rather than political control. They wanted to put responsibility back into the hands of individuals, not take it away.

This theme of personal responsibility ran through activists' recruitment stories and campaigns. Activists first

81

encountered the animal rights movement through its literature and videos. They learned how they had been personally responsible for animal suffering in their former lifestyles—from the leather that covered the soles of their shoes to the factory-farmed meat they bought at the supermarket, from the household products they used to the rodeos and circuses they attended. "Your house was built on land that belonged to animals," a PETA speaker reminded activists at the Animal Rights 101 seminar. "When you drive a car, the motor oil was tested on animals. Every time you look at a photograph, the gelatin on it comes from animals."

Activists described being overwhelmed by guilt and shame over animal cruelty. While some did not use these words, they described feelings we associate with them: "despondence," "depression," and "helplessness." These emotions are self-perpetuating. Guilt about how they hurt animals turned quickly to shame about their own failings. And this shame turned to more guilt for not doing more to overcome their shame.

In finding personal strategies to reconcile their feelings about animal suffering, activists were drawn into larger debates about their relationships with people too. Animal rights campaigns are satirical portrayals of life itself—of the betrayal, detachment, and arrogance that activists see in modern relationships. A few activists had already contemplated these problems as a result of participation in other movements and interpersonal relationships. But to the extent that animal rights activists were trying to reconcile their own feelings in their campaigns, it was their emotions that shaped their moral and political views, not the other way around.

Betrayal

The earliest animal rights campaigns in the state were not against animal research. Instead, they were against the state-run shelters selling abandoned animals to universities for experimentation. This was the issue over which Betty decided to start an animal rights organization. It was also the one that was most bitterly fought over. County commissioners' decisions were overturned and overturned again. The hearings were long, and the speeches impassioned. At its heart were some of the central themes in the animal research controversy.

The animal pound in Springfield County, near the Larger City, had to euthanize over nine thousand abandoned cats and dogs every year. At the height of the breeding season, the staff were putting down fifty-two animals a day. Trucks would take the carcasses to a rendering plant. Cat cadavers would be sold to high schools for dissection. The dogs would become pet-food products for another generation. "They cook 'em down and spin 'em around," a shelter worker told me.

It was obvious to animal researchers that these animals should be used for medical experiments given their undignified ending. And at the time, it made sense to me too. On May 7, 1990, animal researchers sent a delegation of speakers to the county commissioner's office to challenge a previous ruling banning the sale of pound animals to researchers. In the packed court room, a violinist in the Larger City symphony orchestra told of how he was resuscitated from heart failure at the College Town hospital, thanks to techniques practiced on animals from the pound that would otherwise have died for no purpose. And a large, bespectacled veterinarian was outraged that under current laws it was impossible for him to get corneas and tissues even from dead animals at the pound to use for transplants in his veterinary practice.

But the women who led the campaign against the sales did not see trade in pound animals in terms of such benefits. For them, using shelter animals in research represents a betrayal. Pets come to trust humans. Humans fail to reciprocate that trust by abandoning them. Selling them to research represents a double betrayal in which humans not only fail to acknowledge that they have abandoned their pets but also turn them into an expendable commodity. "I just thought about pets," Dee recalled.

They trusted humans and they were very trusting. And through no fault of their own they ended up there. And that's not the purpose of the shelter. The purpose of the shelter is sort of like the end of the line for most animals. They should try to reunite them with their owners. And if that's not possible, they should try to place them in an appropriate home. And if that's not possible, they should euthanize them humanely. So that just bothered me a great deal. It's a cheap source for them. Three dollars for a cat and five for a dog. That's all it was—a cheap source for them.

The apparent willingness of the shelter to turn pets into commodities, to strip them of their status as pets, highlights the fickleness of humans compared with animals. Citing Mark Twain, Dee once said, "You can pick up a starving dog and feed him and make him prosperous, and he will not bite you. This is the principle difference between dog and man."

Betrayal was how another of these early activists, Beryl, viewed animal research itself. Beryl was one of the first activists to arrive at the county commissioners' hearing that day, and we chatted in the lobby waiting for the others. A housewife and part-time receptionist, she first became aware of the animal rights movement when NBC broadcast a story about two chimpanzees that the University of Oklahoma was selling to private laboratories for hepatitis research. She was struck by the fact that this research involved only two animals — chimpanzees with names — rather than the larger numbers of anonymous animals often used in research. A researcher had become emotionally attached to them. Now that the experiments were over, Beryl told me, the university wanted to sell the chimps, thus breaking the emotional bonds and completing the betrayal.

> Their names were Mim and Olive. And they said on the news that they would be in cages for fifty years and injected with hepatitis. What got me about it was the guy who was working on these before was teaching them sign language. He worked with them for ten years. So when they were sold he got all upset. They were so loved. When he came up to them, they ran to him and threw their arms around

him. It showed that on TV. And then it showed how
they would live in a lab.

It is often said, "It is better to have loved and lost, than never
to have loved at all." But Beryl's anguish contradicts this
utilitarian maxim. The severed relationship made the affection all the worse. It was more harmful to experiment on
animals that were once pets, she thought, than animals that
had been specially bred for research: "They don't know
what they're missing."

It was a sad day for the activists when the county commissioners voted, by a narrow majority, to legalize the sale of
pound animals to research. "I've lost all faith in humanity,"
a young preschool teacher called Wendy told me after in
the lobby, her eyes heavy with tears. "Damn," Dee kept
repeating to herself under her breath, flushed with anger.
One of the commissioners she spoke to the night before
had changed his mind and had apparently been persuaded
by the researchers' arguments about the benefits of using
the shelter's animals for research.

For animal rights activists, however, shelters should be
shrines to all the betrayed animals that once lived. In the
words of the animal rights philosopher Tom Regan, they
are a symbol of "our collective irresponsibility" and, like
other "treasured institutions" in the state, should not "be
reducible to dollars and cents."[2] So filled with shame were
people when abandoning animals, that the animal shelter
at the College Town had to set up a specially heated night-
time deposit box for owners to give them up anonymously.
People would rather dump their pets in a sack at the side of

the highway than face the shelter staff in the morning. Keeping pets out of the laboratories meant not only saving the animals from the betrayal of animal research but also being reminded of the betrayal that humans had already perpetrated in abandoning them.

Moreover, in finding benefits from abandoned animals, the scientists were relinquishing the community's responsibility for its pets, according to the activists. In fact, they called the issue "pound seizure." Researchers were literally trying to "seize" the pound from the community. Instead of acknowledging the animals' suffering, researchers were "putting a pretty face" on it. They were trying to mask the betrayal with the benefits of animal research, a point made by a third activist, Shirley.

Shirley was a key speaker on behalf of the animal rights activists at the county commissioners' hearing. "We are not here to discuss the merits of animal research," she reminded the commissioners. "This issue is a Springfield County issue. Others here from outside the county have no business here." The problem, in Shirley's summation, was one of pet overpopulation: "a disease of our own making; a tragedy that deserves much more attention." "No matter how the animals die," she told the commissioners, "we are simply treating the symptom of the disease." Back in her home, Shirley explained to me that all the problems animal rights activists have to deal with go back to the fact that "each individual doesn't do the right thing, doesn't do the little bit of effort it might take on an individual basis to take care of the animals."

This was Shirley's criticism also of how the public deals

with its other problems. The public, for instance, relies too much on medical scientists, rather than looking after their own health.

> They want the medical community to solve all their ills. They want to live just the way they want to live, and then go to the doctors to completely cure them. I think they're looking for a magic potion, and that puts a lot of pressure on doctors to try to find these magic potions.

Most other activists said that they too supported preventive health care so that we wouldn't have to rely on medical scientists or animals. If we didn't eat meat, we wouldn't get heart disease. If we didn't smoke, we wouldn't get cancer. And if we used condoms, we wouldn't get AIDS.

Activists wove this thread of self-reliance into their interpersonal relations. Animals do not rely on others to solve their problems the way that humans do to solve theirs, according to Mary, who joined the Larger City chapter after attending PETA's Animal Rights 101 seminar. "One thing I always hated in my life is how people would eat off me, mentally and emotionally," she said, recalling her college days when other students would knock on her door and tiptoe across the linoleum floors of her dormitory room if they needed help interpreting a piece of poetry they did not understand and she would look up at the ceiling and recite ten different answers for them. "Then, as I grew older, I never liked seeing people who were just going to complain about the men they were dating, or their husbands." She found a purity in the animal rights movement that she had not found in other voluntary organizations or

her relationships with other people. There were people she
knew who considered themselves victims, but they set themselves up to be victimized. The animals did not set themselves up in this way. We victimize them.

> It isn't like they're out spending every night in a
> bar, or they're continually dating men they're go-
> ing to hit on or they're shooting up drugs. I mean,
> they're not doing anything themselves. I feel I
> shouldn't be eating off people, and I shouldn't be
> eating off animals.

Having to wrest responsibility from others makes animal rights activism not just personal but political. The
pound seizure debate, as its name suggests, became a fight
for responsibility. It was, in the words of sociologist Joseph
Gusfield, a contest for the ownership of a public problem.[3]
Animal rights activists wanted the problem of animal cruelty, like illness and disease, to be in the hands of the individuals whom they saw as responsible for it — not scientists
or shelter boards. Aside from selling animals to research,
there were other ways that activists saw people relinquishing their responsibility for animals, in the very act of detaching themselves from them.

Detachment

After watching their first animal rights movies, activists
reflected on how they themselves had earlier in their lives
stripped animals of their petlike qualities. Most obviously,
they had turned animals into "food," cows into "beef,"
and pigs into "pork." Comfortably anesthetized by mod-

ern means of production, the animal rights activists reflected, we have become insensitive to animal suffering.
Animal cruelty no longer appears as an isolated, accidental
occurrence. It is "sanctioned," "systematized," and "institutionalized" by a society that routinely strips animals of
their sentience.

This situation was brought to life for Douglas, the founder and coordinator of the College Town chapter, in the
animal rights movie *The Animals Film*. Douglas grew up on
his father's feudal estate in Germany, where he spent his
youth hunting. He left Germany for the United States with
the hope of becoming a concert pianist. Insecure about his
talent as a virtuoso, he played for the ballet, nightclubs,
and movies before getting married and taking up a more
stable occupation as a computer programmer. Tall, white
haired, and distinguished, with a deep Germanic voice,
Douglas "drifted into" animal rights when his wife, Lucille,
began to volunteer with the local humane society shelter
on Kennedy Road. At night over dinner, Lucille would tell
him about the litters of cats and dogs that the shelter staff
found abandoned at the side of the road or left in parking
lots and dumpsters. Lucille rose to be president of the
shelter and defended its decision not to sell abandoned
animals to research. One night, she organized a seminar to
which she invited officials in the animal protection community. She ended her presentation by showing *The Animals Film*.

Douglas describes that evening as the "turning point"
in becoming an animal rights activist. In vivid detail, he still
recalls the movie that brought him to tears: A worker in a

chicken processing plant sits for eight hours a day doing nothing but operating a machine that melts away chickens' beaks with a red hot iron in order to prevent them from hacking each other to death in the close confines of their cages. The man is so detached from the animals that he casually takes his lunch after cutting off two thousand beaks and then comes back for more. Douglas was so overwrought by what he had seen that he had to leave the room. He sat outside, pale and shivering in the dim light. "I knew my life would never be the same," he told me. Douglas was drawn into the movie. He saw himself as part of the system, a cog in the machine of animal abuse. "I, at least, cannot be part of this anymore," he recalled thinking to himself. "I was part of it simply because of my ignorance."

As a hunter, Douglas had seen animals suffer before. But the victims of the aristocratic hunting tradition in which he grew up were protected by a "hunter's honor code" that acknowledged the animals' suffering.

> If you wound a deer, it's your obligation to see if it is dead. And if it's not, you must immediately give it a second shot and put it out of its misery because to allow the animal to suffer is very much against the hunter's ethics. It bugged me a little. But I thought these are occasional aberrations. They're not really part of the whole design.

The vast numbers of animals on factory farms and in research laboratories that Douglas saw in the film, however, were not protected by this code.

When I saw the system where billions of animals are routinely treated every year in this manner: where their entire lives are spent in agony and misery in those big systems such as factory farming and the trapping industry and in laboratories, especially military research and cosmetic research for such frivolous reasons as lipstick and nail polish, and the agony that the rabbit had to go through — that had an enormous emotional impact on me.

Other activists, who had also grown up in hunting communities, confirmed Douglas's feelings. The hunter, according to Stanley, is different from the person who buys his meat from the supermarket because he gets to see what happens to the animals. He gets to empathize, even suffer with them. The factory farmer and the consumer of plastic-wrapped meat from the supermarkets or McDonald's do not.

The detachment of humans from animals reminds Stanley of a Nazi-like world that encourages ordinary people, like himself, to commit cruel acts against innocent others. Like factory farming, animal research — which processes large numbers of animals with no individual identity — epitomizes this detachment. Stanley's first animal rights video, *The Hidden Holocaust*, reminded him of a period in his life after college when he took a job as a technician in an animal research laboratory. It was this detachment that turned him into an animal abuser. Hooking up animals to machines, cutting off their toes, and bleeding them to death, he began to see the Nazi in himself.

I literally started thinking to myself, reading about Joseph Mengele and what he did and tying it all together. I started thinking to myself when I would go downstairs and get my rats from the building and bring them upstairs: This is what they did in Germany. People just taking these creatures and detaching themselves. To do the surgical procedures you have to be detached. In fact the first thing I ever did—at the first lab I ever worked in back in Illinois—was to toe clip with no anesthesia to identify the animals. I thought it was pretty crazy. But like I say, you buy into it pretty quickly because you're told that they don't bleed a whole lot. And at first they scream. But as soon as you put them down, they kind of walk around and limp. But they look OK if you go back an hour later. They might be licking their paw, but they basically look OK. And you start to accept that as the price you pay to do the research to get the benefits.

Stanley had always cared about animals. He was the activist who never understood why the kids in his neighborhood threw rocks at cats. Long before animal rights became a public issue in the state, he was a member of the humane society and the Fund for Animals. The longer he was in animal research, the worse he felt about it. "It got to the point where I felt ashamed of what I was doing," he told me. "When people would ask me what I did, I would jokingly say, 'I beat up on animals all day.' And I got to the point where I realized that that was my way of getting through my own guilt—to try to joke about it." After *The Hidden Holocaust*, Stanley could no longer live with the guilt.

Activists reflected on this detachment in other aspects of their lives. Beryl's husband, Jim, who owns a furniture company, described the world of business in terms of a game of poker, where you are encouraged to hold your cards to your chest.

> People have a tendency not to tell you how they feel about anything because it's a protection mechanism. Especially in business. That's what you've been taught. In business you are there to come out of a negotiation with an advantage. So the less the individual knows about your workings and the things that bother you the better. Like poker players. You don't know what's going on. You don't know when you've hit the hot button and when you haven't. It's a game.

For Jim, talking about animal rights was a way to encourage George, one of the people he does business with, to express his feelings.

> It opens up a conversation about the environment, about life in general—what his aspirations and hopes are and what mine are. And you begin to talk about something that's a little more real than what you're accustomed to. The only way you can talk about these issues is to interject your personal feelings. You find out what's behind the mask.

Like the Victorian antivivisectionists, the two mothers I interviewed worry particularly about children becoming detached. Requiring high school students to dissect animals, they fear, encourages this attitude. They persuaded their children's school teachers to adopt alternative teaching methods. "Requiring high-school dissections," one of their leaflets warns, "may be very detrimental to students in that it teaches them insensitivity. This is contrary to what is taught in all other school disciplines—respect for life." According to another pamphlet:

> The most important thing to remember about the use of animals in medical school training is that it desensitizes students. If they're going to be doctors, medical school students need to be sensitive. Half the battle in diagnosing and treating illness and disease lies in the doctor's sensitivity to his patients.

The animal rights movement provided ways for these activists to be sensitive to animals, to pay respect to the animals through their empathy. We often believe, as sociologist Arlie Hochschild suggests, that we owe others our feelings.[4] Feelings are like gifts. Just as traditional societies exchange shells and beads for friendship and we reciprocate dinner invitations, so we trade feelings with one another. In this sense, the hunter pays his "emotional dues" to the animals; the factory farmer and animal researcher do not. Through the animal rights movement, activists could constantly remind themselves of animal suffering. Animals Anon staged funerals for animals killed for fur or animal research. One activist imagined what it must be like to be experimented on, as he read about animal research in animal rights literature. Another made regular visits to an abattoir to remind herself of the cruelty involved in eating meat. And Shirley forced herself to watch animal rights videos. "It is very hard to look at," she admitted.

> Pictures and TV shows and movies and things. I mean it makes me cry. And it's not that I'm a sadist or a masochist or whatever. But I really believe it's true that if the animals endure these things at our hands, if they have to live through it or die through it, then the least we can do is watch. It's real painful at times. But that's how you learn. I think most people just kind of put up that wall and don't let themselves look at it very hard.

Shirley tried to acknowledge the animals' suffering by suffering with them or, as Hochschild puts it, by paying her emotional dues.

Such detachment was exacerbated for most activists by institutional arrangements that made animals private property for which the owners remained unaccountable. They let their pets wander the street. They beat them or left them chained to a fence all day. Researchers, most of all, kept animals behind closed doors — a situation continually confirmed by activists' frustrations in trying to find out details about animal experiments at their local universities. "It's shown how powerful the bureaucracy can be," Shirley explained. "And it really points out the fact that researchers can do whatever they want to, that they aren't truly accountable for what they do." As private property, animals became untouchable, invisible, and isolated from the community.

Those who fought the universities rationalized that it was not just the animals that were privately owned. The

universities, like the animals, had become private property—a position most strongly articulated by Arnold. Arnold was a graduate student in the College Town when I
met him. He was absorbed in a thesis on Marxism, critical
theory, and deconstructionism that I could never understand. But he was clearly influenced by the left. For Arnold,
Ronald Reagan allowed the universities to be taken over by
the "private interests" of large corporations, encouraging
them to become purely profit-seeking institutions rather
than serving the public. The animal rights movement allowed Arnold to take back the power from these groups.

It's giving me an understanding and appreciation
of what really being a socially active responsible
agent is all about. It's given me a feel for participa-
tory grass-roots democracy. Something I've never
really experienced before — this feeling that damn!
The five of us sitting here, we can make a difference. We can put pressure on multi-million dollar
interests. We can reach the public.

Animal rights activism reinforced Arnold's democratic
values and gave him a way to put his political ideals into
practice. But Arnold's activism was far more personal than
protesting multi-million-dollar interests. In his own neighborhood, he began to attend to things that he ordinarily
would not have. I recall, for instance, an afternoon driving
back with Arnold and his wife from a Rosenthal protest. We
hit the outskirts of the College Town—a no-man's land of
automobile repair shops, laundromats, and dreary diners.
A small retriever scurried across the street, stopping to
sniff at the long tufts of grass sprouting out of the cracks

between the concrete where the curb met the tarmac. Arnold put his foot on the brake pedal and turned to his wife. "What do you think?" he asked. "Does he know where he's going?" If the dog was lost, Arnold explained, he would take it to the pound and the owners would have to pay thirty dollars to reclaim it. Even if he knew who the owners were, he would still take an animal to the pound so that they would be fined for their negligence. In effect, Arnold had set up his own little animal police patrol in which he would go around the leafy neighborhoods to ensure that his neighbors looked after their animals.

Most activists prefer these individual acts to large protests. The personal is easier to control than the political, no matter how great the sacrifice. I always thought, for instance, that vegetarianism requires tremendous discipline. I struggled with it for many years myself. Yet all but two of the activists that I interviewed are strict vegetarians. And many of them described "overnight vegetarianism." "We can't always control what happens to the animals, but we can at least control what we eat," Dee announced at a vegetarian Thanksgiving meal in the Larger City. And what about the two activists who do eat meat? They did not discredit the animal rights philosophy for demanding impossible moral standards. Instead they blamed themselves for their own personal failings — "a weakness in me."

Arrogance

Irresponsibility comes from another personal failing — arrogance. It is arrogant, according to the activists, to pick and choose which animals should be loved, eaten, or exper-

imented on. Shirley described humans as "playing God" in
their relationships with animals, while another activist went
as far as to describe humans as "a cancer taking over and de-
stroying everything in its path." Everywhere, activists found
evidence of our arrogance toward animals. Animals occupy
the light-hearted stories at the end of the news. Ordinances
surrounding animal cruelty group animals with plants. The
"fringe" image of the animal rights movement reminds
activists that there is no one to speak for the animals. The
animals are alone in their pain. Human arrogance is particularly evident in the way we sacrifice animals for our own
benefit, despite the fact that they have qualities similar or
even superior to our own. As we sat in Shirley's living room
one afternoon, her cats curling about our legs, Shirley reflected on the trivial and meaningless existence of her own
suburban life compared to those of her pets.

> We look at these cats wandering around here and
> think: "Well, you know, they can't think about all
> these lofty ideas, and their life really consists of
> eating and sleeping and playing and being petted.
> That's certainly not really as worthy a life as what
> I do, which is get up and drink coffee full of caf-
> feine and eat my fat-laden meals and smoke my ciga-
> rettes and go to a job that I hate and make all this
> money, so I can live in a bigger house and drive a
> bigger car." People somehow think that that makes
> us more worthy. For me, cats' lives are simpler, but
> in some ways they sound better.

Shirley and all the other activists were quick to remind
me that we take the goodness of animals for granted: We

betray one another, but animals are loyal. We overpopulate and pollute, but animals regulate their populations. We make nuclear weapons and wage wars, but animals live in harmony with one another. We kill for greed, but animals kill for survival. Douglas once said that even earthworms, amoebae, and microbes—"the little creatures"—have their role to play.

> If humans died out tomorrow, the earth would not only not suffer but it would begin to recover. But if all the earthworms died out tomorrow, nothing would fertilize the soil. The earth would be injured irreparably. So therefore the little creatures, the amoebae, the microbes are more important than the humans.

For the pound seizure protesters, animal experimentation epitomized our arrogance. Scientists are supposed to be prestigious and knowledgeable—most of all about animals. But instead of showing humility, they were playing God by picking and choosing who lives and who dies. "What all of animal rights amounts to," Shirley explained, "research in particular, is not a question of whether killing a hundred cats or dogs or whatever benefits humans, but is the benefit really the point? Who are we to say if our life is more valuable and really deserves the sacrifice of other creatures?" Betty's experiences as an English professor confirmed the researchers' arrogance. She recalled the space race of the 1960s, when it was difficult for the English Department to get money because it was all being funneled into the sciences. Scientists were taking resources away

from society's more fundamental needs. "They want prestige, they want to impress others," she said.

> They make out that their work is beneficial to oth-
> ers; that their work is so important that it uses the
> most valuable materials. Often scientists don't have
> a well-balanced background. They don't read liter-
> ature, sociology, and history. They do not have an
> awareness of the values that support civilization,
> that support mankind.

In the 1990s, money was short again. The state was undergoing budget cuts. Animal research at the prestigious universities was, according to another activist, diverting money
from children's schooling and community colleges.

Nothing represents human arrogance more than wearing fur or animal-tested cosmetics. The campaigns I observed against fur and cosmetics testing included some
of the richest symbolism and slogans. Activists who ran
them played heavily on images of beauty at the expense of
pain. They staged a funeral for fur, with an undertaker and
coffin; "No Beauty Without Brutality," "Beauty and the
Beast," literature and newsletters proclaimed. At their most
daring, activists dressed in flesh-colored tights and leotards
to appear naked. Taking an animal's skin implied sexual
violation. They obsessed with almost erotic fascination with
how pain and beauty intertwine. One man came back from
a meeting with Rosenthal appalled by her cruelty but impressed by her youth and attractiveness. Part of her arrogance seemed to come from her good looks. In fact,
some of the threats against Rosenthal were overtly sexual.

She showed me one letter in which an anonymous activist threatened to mutilate her genitals, as if stomping out her sexuality would stomp out her power.

A kind of asceticism pervaded the activists' own lives. They wore jeans and T-shirts. They rarely used makeup. Some activists did not wear leather, although they saw it as less decadent than fur — a "by-product" of meat. One leaflet not only advised against wearing fur but waxed sour about wearing imitations: "Buy fake fur, if you *must* have the 'look.'" Activists see fur as arrogance at the expense of other people, not just animals. "Money. Elegance. Elaborateness," Betty spat the words out while showing me literature from the Fur Information Council. "Fur," she explained, "is a symbol of those kinds of things. Emphasis on appearances, on superficialities — how you get to have prestige in our society. The assumption that people have values in that direction rather than in a moral direction: brotherhood, sensitivity, and education."

Activists began to notice arrogance in other aspects of their lives. They criticized organized religion, particularly Judaism and Christianity, for promoting arrogance by encouraging worshippers to think that they are superior to one another, as well as to animals. Only Stanley attended church regularly, and his church promoted a liberal, Unitarian philosophy. Activists who did talk about religion with me preferred doctrines in which God lives "within" rather than above people. One woman had come to believe that God is an energy, rather than an entity — not "some master being sitting up there doing whatever he's doing, dancing around in the clouds up there." After becoming an animal rights activist, another woman thought that religion

should be concerned with "concepts such as love and discipline, being connected to the universe, not wanting to hurt
anything, living in harmony, respecting earth, respecting
each other." Unlike these activists, Beryl said that she actually drew closer to her southern Baptist upbringing after
joining the movement. The movement had taught her
compassion, which she believed is at the heart of Christianity. In focusing on this aspect of the religion, animal
rights activism could reinforce Christianity, just as it reinforced the alternative conceptions of God held by the
other activists. All activists, however, agreed that the same
kind of one-upmanship that humans exhibit toward animals is responsible for humans' exploitation of other humans. Mary's boyfriend spoke for most activists when he
told me:

> I think people in this world — be they researchers
> or not — they want to feel better. And the way they
> feel better is to step on or get up above a black,
> above a woman, above a poor person, above an
> uneducated person. There are people who will put
> down other people just to make themselves feel
> better. If you want to equate it with researchers, I
> think researchers want the power, want the pres-
> tige, want the money to get ahead, and that is the
> field they've chosen in which to do that.

Activists, then, did not want to put animals above humans
in a hierarchy. It was hierarchy that they criticized. Precisely because we have more technological know-how and
intelligence than animals, we should not be arrogant. "If
we've got this brain," Shirley explained, "and can reason

and think and have the ability to do so much good, then along with that should go compassion and conscience to hold that in check." With power should come compassion for animals. In fact, in my conversations with activists, the word *compassion* came up whenever they talked about arrogance. Compassion is an antidote to arrogance.

Animal rights literature and campaigns allowed activists to show compassion toward animals. It allowed them to express deference and humility toward them, sometimes to the point of sanctifying them in religious ways. An anti-hunting pamphlet quotes Joseph Wood Krutch as saying that animals are "the works of God." Activists took part in an entire religious service for animals, "The Blessing of the Animals." They brought their pets to the steps of a local chapel, where banners reminded the congregation of activists and news reporters "the Lord God made them all." A rabbi and a priest read biblical stories about animals and led the congregation in singing "All Things Bright and Beautiful." A young man recounted the story of Saint Francis, who was "always very kind and wonderfully compassionate, especially toward gentle animals and little birds." Even though many activists were cynical about organized religion, they turned to God to show their humility.

In the animal rights movement, activists are forced to deal with the contradictions of a previous life in which they both exploited animals and kept them as pets. Maintaining the pounds as a refuge for animals helped the early Animals Anon campaigners show their loyalty to animals in the face of betrayal. Watching animal rights movies helped them empathize with the animals in the face of detachment. And protesting fur helped them show humility to the animals in the face of arrogance. "What I like most about it," Shirley said, "is I feel I'm doing something to help. It's probably a very selfish kind of reason. But at least it makes me feel better. At least I'm not just sitting back and saying, 'Yes, it's terrible. But there's nothing I can do about it.' It makes me feel powerful, like I'm doing something."

Reluctantly, however, activists found their personal struggles entangled with political ones: against universities, animal dealers, factory farms, furriers, fast food franchises, and pet owners. While activists could control their own actions, they could not control those of others. Having learned about the causes of animal cruelty, activists found themselves at odds not just with their own treatment of animals or cruel individuals but with whole organizations, industries, and society itself. Like a thread, the more one pulls at it, the looser it becomes; previously held cultural categories fell away. It was no longer possible, for instance, to morally distinguish between companion animals and food animals. What began as a concern for pets ended in a critique of modern relationships and lifestyles.

It was here that social organization intervened. Activists, particularly leaders, who bore the brunt of the work, became overwhelmed with the magnitude of animal cruelty. Betty had devoted a whole room in her house to animal rights activism. Filing cabinets were wedged in every corner, brimming with animal rights literature and newspaper clippings, and the walls were lined with shelves of videos. She had been spending six hours a day on animal rights activism. Similarly, the Farm raid had a profound effect on Saul and his young wife. "Our lives became very disrupted," she recalled.

> I mean it was literally phone calls continuously. It felt like from the minute we got home from work there would be people calling. And we might be sitting down to eat and somebody would call and Saul would get wrapped up in a conversation and could be on the phone for hours. The newspapers were calling, the radio, PETA, people from around the state.

When I attended my last meeting in 1992, most of the core activists that I write about here had stepped back from the movement and rarely came to meetings.[5]

It was easy to start campaigns. As members of a non-profit group, organizers could advertise free in the local newspapers and on public radio. Postage was free, too. A protest with ten to fifteen people and a few props, such as candles and costumes, could put them on the six o'clock news, or at least get them a mention and a photograph in the local newspaper, one of the main sources of recruitment for Animals Anon. And mass-produced, preprinted postcards made a letter-writing campaign against Rosenthal's research a relatively low-cost affair. The activists themselves were surprised at how easy it was to draw publicity and alarm the researchers.

But activists had difficulty sustaining these campaigns. The students in the College Town eventually won their lawsuit to inspect animal research proposals. They also negotiated with the administrators to walk the laboratory dogs. Shortly after these victories, however, Saul graduated from the university, and the student organization folded. No one ever showed up at the labs to walk the dogs, and no proposals were ever inspected. "It's a real shame," he lamented at the church hall one night. "It would be unfair to the dogs to get them used to grass and walks, then to stop." A further betrayal. A national animal rights organization had declared the following Saturday World Day for Laboratory Animals, and Saul was now having to look around for animal abuses at the other universities to, as he put it, "relieve our collective guilt for not doing anything."

Taking part in animal rights campaigns helped activists overcome their guilt and shame. But it could also exacerbate these feelings. In the animal rights movement, the more one does, the more one finds one has to do, like a Russian doll that you open to find more dolls waiting. "You begin to look at what people eat, at what you eat. You begin to look at how people treat animals, how people talk about animals," Linda, an attorney in the College Town, recalls of her early experiences in the movement. "What gives me the boost is knowing that if I sit down and relax—which I do a lot—or I do something I want to do, there are animals suffering. They don't get to walk away."

Five

Stewardship and Science

Animal researchers, when recalling their earliest experiments, identified with the animal rights activists' feelings of guilt over animal use. Even Animals Anon's most ardent opponents did so. When Rachel Rosenthal began her training in the 1960s, she already knew that animal research is a "crime," for she had always been taught that humans and animals are biologically related. This was long before the modern animal rights movement was under way.

> I remember the first day when I walked into the lab. I'd gotten in after the experiment began, so I was confronted with a cat that was anesthetized in a stereotaxic apparatus. It had its scalp open and the skull was exposed. And I remember just kind of, HUHHHH! Feeling kind of a physical impact. And remarking to myself that if you believe in the continuity of organisms in the evolutionary sense, then we are different to cats, but only in degree. This was in the early 1960s before any of the animal rights stuff had come out. So if it was a crime to do re-

search on people, it was only a lesser crime — but
nonetheless a crime — to do it to animals.

Cathy O'Brien, the College Town psychologist, identified
with the guilty emotions that the activists felt as well as the
moral view that went with it. She felt more like the animal
rights activists than unlike them: "I recognized myself in a
lot of people who were being captivated by this movement.
They were people whom I could identify with. I consider
myself a politically and socially very progressive person."
She saw in the U.S. army in Vietnam the same kind of
detachment that animal rights activists read into animal
research.

> The scientific establishment looks to them like a
> symbol of entrenched power and authority. Kind
> of callous and mechanistic — you know — like how I
> saw the army when I was a kid during the Vietnam
> era. I am very much a 1960s type of person. I could
> see being in their shoes.

The way researchers deal with their feelings about animal research, however, is more complex than just an appeal to the benefits of science, as animal rights activists
assume. Instead, they see science itself as a way of paying
emotional dues to the animals.

Responsibility

Like the animal rights activists, animal researchers
spoke about responsibility. They saw animal research as
fulfilling a responsibility to preserve life. Humans have

been endowed with a certain role in nature to help or protect. Humans and, in particular, scientists have an obligation to fulfill this role. O'Brien and others described this role as "stewardship." O'Brien recognized it in her own work.

O'Brien was studying Alzheimer's disease in rats when I met her. Old rats have poor memories, like Alzheimer's patients. And, like Alzheimer's patients, these rats exhibit a strange protein called beta amyloid that clots in large plaques in their brains. But O'Brien believed that some of these old rats, which had better memories than the others, had found a way to destroy the protein. The research was exciting — articles in *Science* and *Nature* were filled with talk about beta amyloid — and O'Brien was deeply moved by the plight of Alzheimer's patients. The disease takes an appalling toll on the lives of those who suffer from it. Patients, she explained, literally lose touch with their identity. It is slow, progressive, and ends in death. And it is twice as devastating for those who have to care for these patients. O'Brien described science, including her own research, as "a human impulse to want to conserve life using whatever means are available."

> I'm not satisfied with the condition where, you know, I have ten babies and three survive. I want to protect all children who are born. Humans have the capacity to engage in that kind of protective enterprise — which is far more vast than standing in front of the lair and fending off the predators. We can actually think about the causes of the disease and understand them. We *can* gain knowledge about

some of the things that are affecting our well being
and our ability to survive.

While both animal rights activists and animal researchers talked about responsibility, each side had a different
understanding of what it meant. The animal rights activists
described responsibility as individuals curbing their own
actions so that they do not hurt others — a kind of personal
etiquette. But O'Brien spoke of a much more grand and
paternalistic kind of responsibility. For her and other scientists, responsibility meant fulfilling a role that had been
assigned to them to protect those who could not protect
themselves — "protecting all the children that are born."
Through science, human beings can "tinker with nature"
to improve it. It is therefore incumbent upon them to do
so. To animal rights activists, however, this thinking represented arrogance.

Like the animal rights activists, animal researchers
found resonance for their view in religious beliefs. But
whereas most animal rights activists found little solace in
conventional religion because of its seemingly arrogant
hierarchies, researchers found support for human stewardship in Judeo-Christian traditions. O'Brien, a Catholic,
noted:

> I think it may be rooted in my religious education.
> In fact it's deeply rooted in all my life experiences. I
> see humans as having a distinctive role to play in
> the world. It has to do with stewardship. It has to do
> with our great capacity to do harm and also our
> great capacity for doing good. I don't expect a fox
> or other animals to take on this responsibility or

stewardship. But I do expect humans to do this and to make ethical decisions.

In this respect, animal researchers found great affinity with other protectionist endeavors, including strains of environmentalism. Biological studies of ecology, a zoologist noted in a local radio debate with animal rights activists, exemplifies man's appropriate stewardship of nature, which is neither arrogant nor irresponsible.

> We must avoid the arrogant superiority that has been claimed by humans in the past and see what our rightful place is on the planet earth—which is not a position that justifies the mindless exploitation of everything that we can get our hands on. Indeed, it seems to me that we biologists have probably been light years ahead of those of you who have recently discovered nature in speaking up for the preservation of this planet and in acknowledging man's position in an intricate network of living forms that he does not and should not control.

Yet researchers' belief in stewardship led most to somewhat conservative conclusions when they were defending themselves against animal rights activists. If science is a way of taking responsibility for life, then scientists are the ones who should make decisions about using animals in experiments. Decisions about medical research, according to Harold Finch, the laboratory veterinarian at a nearby medical school, "must be resolved in the laboratory by scientific methodology, or established by those qualified experts in science. They cannot be resolved in the arena of public debate." Researchers did not intend for comments like this to sound elitist—merely practical. One takes one's medical problems to a medical scientist for treatment, just as one takes one's car to an automobile mechanic for repair. For animal rights activists, the ethicist and scientist resides within everyone. But for animal researchers, being responsible means adhering to a division of labor in which scientists have the last word in ethical issues surrounding animal experimentation.

Rationality

The researchers I spoke to acknowledged that not all human use of animals is responsible; there is potential for humans to be both good and bad. "Knowledge is an ambiguous thing," as several put it. Good animal research must be "rational" or "appropriate."[1] Ironically, it was often emotions that distinguished the good from the bad animal experiments.

The distinction between appropriate and inappropriate animal research sometimes hinges on the traditional professional distinction between pure and commercial science. Commercial research—"technology" in O'Brien's classification—is motivated by money. Animal research undertaken at universities—"science"—is motivated by the preserving impulse.

> Product testing is technology. There's no science to that. And it's driven by a system that is basically economic. You want to sell things, but you don't want to get sued should anything happen. And so

these tests are done. You've brought your insurance policy against the public launching suits and holding manufacturers responsible for all the consequences of the things that they make and sell.

Four other researchers were also against product testing because they, like the animal rights activists, viewed it as a nonessential, even extravagant use of animals.

In drawing boundaries between appropriate and inappropriate animal research, animal researchers further distinguished among practitioners of their own profession. Most said that they knew of, although had never met, animal researchers who were cruel to animals. For David Nathan, these "butchers," like the Pennsylvania head-injury researchers, were more common in the past than now—the back street abortionists of the animal research world.

I think there have been some biomedical researchers that have been butchers in the past. In human nature, in any endeavor, you've got a range of qualities from the worst to the very best. It applies to surgery. You've got some surgeons who have been butchers and murderers too. So you can't characterize anything that involves human beings as uniformly pure.

Because of new regulations and heightened publicity over animal research, such cruelty, he thought, is unlikely to happen again. In other instances, researchers portrayed cruel scientists as psychopaths. Henry Weiss, the immunologist on the College Town Institutional Animal Care and Use Committee (IACUC), once said:

I find a lot of reports of cruelty to be about patho-
logical individuals. I think that the stories you hear
are often of somebody who's really unbalanced.
That individual may have a Ph.D., and they may be
a researcher. But the times that I've seen where
I agree that there was cruelty to animals, I think
these are asocial people who need care. I mean
they are just not normal people.

In other cases, researchers were known to be cruel to animals out of ignorance rather than intent. At the College
Town university and the research institute, foreign lab assistants broke rules about euthanizing animals because,
according to the head veterinarian, there was no culture of
animal care in their home countries. "They think that rats
are just something you step on or throw around," he commented, only half jokingly.

Such situations are rare, but admittedly difficult to control. Consequently, like animal rights activism, responsible
animal research comes down to very personal decisions. All
but two researchers talked about limits to what they would
or would not do or accept in animal experimentation. Researchers had the most reservations about experiments
with infant animals. It is widely known that a researcher at
the College Town university, the mother of several children, will not experiment with baby rats. Another woman, a
university administrator, admitted that she finds descriptions of maternal deprivation experiments to be "really
painful." The veterinarian at the College Town university
shared this view. O'Brien said that while she would never be
a subject for her own experiments, she always takes all the

precautions and gives the aftercare she would expect if she was having the surgery done on herself. Other researchers had similar "do unto others" policies. At the institute, researchers would not kill an animal while in the presence of other animals for fear it would traumatize them, even though this was not specified in the National Institutes of Health regulations. Such choices extend to researchers' lives outside their occupation. Nathan would never buy a fur coat for his wife; one researcher was even a vegetarian.

Refusing to appear moved by personal qualms, other researchers sought to equate animal cruelty with bad science when defending animal experiments. If animals are suffering, according to this view, the scientific data would be invalid. "Animal experimentation to study injury gives me real problems," Nathan admitted. "I think we need to understand how the human body works in its natural state, rather than try to find out what happens if you beat it to death," he explained. "Only a stupid scientist is going to use animals that are not well cared for," according to Gabe Johnson, a pediatrician in the College Town. One IACUC member carefully framed it this way:

> As a scientist, if I wanted to defend my position to someone who has absolutely no care about what is happening to animals, this would be one argument I would use: If an animal is experiencing discomfort or pain, and that is not critical to the project — that is, you are not studying the physiological response to pain — chances are your data is not going to be very good, because there are all sorts of physiological changes that accompany animals in distress.

Such beliefs reinforce the idea that science is innately responsible, if practiced well. In reality, however, researchers could not separate their personal feelings from scientific practice in this way. Science is an inherently emotional undertaking in its commitment to preserving life. Animal research is, as Finch put it, an "awesome responsibility." Rosenthal felt this responsibility more than anyone else I met, perhaps because she more than anyone else knew what it was like to spend hours working on a live cat with its spine exposed.

> Any time I begin an experiment I have to carry on my shoulders a certain moral weight. And that weight infuses the way I do my experiments. If the experiments are going badly, the data might not be any good now, the graduate students are tired, you're tired, and you've got the cat out on the table committed — the point is that once you begin an experiment, your personal comfort is irrelevant. Not only do we have to finish the experiment, we owe it to the animal to finish it. You have as your primary moral obligation, once you're committed, to finish the experiment. If you don't, you've violated your trust with the animal who has to commit wholeheartedly, so to speak, with no return.

Animal rights activists, in this respect, appear irresponsible. They reap the benefits of animal use without taking responsibility for the moral costs. "There's kind of a fraud going on," Rosenthal said, referring to cruelty-free cosmetics whose ingredients, she believed, had already been tested on animals.

It's a kind of moral self-indulgence on the part of the public, where they can have the moral purity without any of the costs of making the moral decision — like getting someone else to hold an umbrella while you claim the moral purity of never having to avoid the rain.

Isolation

Rosenthal's story belies the sense of alienation I found among targeted researchers. Like animal rights activists, animal researchers and their supporters also talked about isolation in the community. Animal rights activists spoke of their detachment from animals, from one another, and from increasingly privatized public institutions. Researchers and their supporters similarly alluded to a "communication gap," "misunderstanding," or "confusion" that had arisen between them and those who protest animal experiments, along with more general misconceptions held by the public about what scientists do and who they are. Researchers felt isolated in a second way too. They felt isolated from other medical professionals who had not come to their defense. "Everybody's been out there fighting their own battle," as Nathan put it.

But we're all fighting the same battle. Because the local physicians don't get attacked, they don't respond. Because the local veterinarians don't get attacked, they don't respond. The local Diabetes Association, they don't respond. We need to convince them that they are being attacked. The very

body of knowledge on which they base their clinical
work with patients is being attacked.

This detachment has several sources, according to the
researchers. The specialized nature of animal research itself compounds the public's skepticism. Animal research
cannot be explained within the thirty-second sound-bites
that television news shows afford them. "We speak a different language," Finch lamented in a speech at a symposium on animal research. "It's hard for us to explain
what we're doing." It is difficult, Nathan agreed, to defend
animal research that goes on in a laboratory when the public never gets to see the results. The public does not trust
animal researchers, only those who apply their results. "We
need to have the public hear from the people they trust,"
Nathan suggested, "namely, the physicians they go to when
they're sick, the veterinarians they take their pets to, the
Diabetes Association they're giving contributions to, and
the business associations."

Another source of isolation came from the animal rights
movement itself. Animal rights spokespersons had become
very skilled at arguing against animal researchers. By researchers' own accounts, scientists were less persuasive in
public. Close to World Day for Laboratory Animals, for instance, the Channel Five News Network ran a special feature on the animal research controversy. They invited the
psychologist Neal Bernard from the animal rights movement to speak out against animal research. Johnson agreed
to debate him. Bernard began talking about brain injury
research at Tulane University that involved shooting cats in
the head. He dismissed the research as useless. Johnson

knew little about these particular experiments and could not defend them, so he attacked Bernard's qualifications. It would have been better, he thought later, to have pointed out how useful brain injury research is. Bernard had exploited the specialized nature of science and by Johnson's own admission made him look stupid. Not only was Bernard adept with facts, but as the public relations woman for the National Association of Biomedical Research pointed out, "he was very young-looking, very attractive, and highly articulate." After that, researchers were afraid to take part in television debates. They felt isolated when they did not speak out. But they felt even more isolated when they did.

Animal rights activists not only denied researchers their technical expertise but denied them their emotions too. Going back to Rosenthal's moral burden, Rosenthal resented the fact that those who criticized her did so without knowing about the weight she carried: "I don't like the idea of people who have never carried that weight recriminating me, as if they're the first ones who have thought of this, and I'm some heartless monster that hasn't." Nathan admitted to me that he supported the animal rights movement on some issues: their opposition to the head-injury experiments, cosmetics testing, and fur coats. But he also knew that he would give the animal rights movement credit if he expressed these reservations in public, thus betraying his research colleagues.

Researchers' sense of isolation again led them and their supporters to conservative conclusions about the public and science. They reflected not just on the animal rights movement but on a broader trend in American society in which the public has become increasingly cynical about science — "a closing of the American mind" — one researcher said, quoting the social critic Allan Bloom. The animal rights movement is "riding a tide of anti-intellectual, pseudo-scientific fanaticism that has a much broader-based appeal than most doctors would credit," according to a writer in the *Southern Physician*, the local medical doctor's journal. A biologist at the university in the Larger City described a "sorry state of affairs" in which the current generation of children is being raised on an "unhealthy diet of horoscopes and magic pyramids." Captivated by the hot tabloid titillation of commercial television, the current generation, according to Johnson, has no use for the science documentaries on public television: "You get some marvelous programs about biomedical research, ethics, and all that stuff. Who watches it? Nobody. It's not sexy. It's not entertaining. It's not fun."

Whereas animal rights activists saw the 1960s as a time when science was consuming too much of the federal budget, animal researchers saw it as the beginning of an "anti-science" movement. Rosenthal was a graduate student then. She recalled how her friends in graduate school, particularly those who married outside of academia, lived in communes. At home they were living like hunters and gatherers, shunning anything technological. This puzzled Rosenthal. It stood in contradiction to their studies. "There was this sense," she recalled, "in which what they did professionally ran counter to the zeitgeist of the community in which they operated, which was really strongly anti-intellectual, anti-technology." Compared with animal rights activists, animal researchers spoke cynically about the 1960s in general. Three of them were part of the sixties protests. But now, in the context of the animal rights movement, they distanced themselves from it. When the Southern Christian Leadership Conference gained momentum, Rosenthal and her friends tried to form a civil rights organization in Texas, where she was an undergraduate. But she said she was peripheral to the movement. The university's lawyer, Mable Payne, was empathetic with the sixties protesters but now sees them as churlish.

> I'm a person who came of age in the sixties. That's when I was in college, the early sixties. I went through the Vietnam era and behaved like many people in those days in making your views known, wanting to be heard. This was part of the culture. In the case of the war, people protested the war. In the case of civil rights, people protested institutionalized segregation. So I'm part of that generation. And I learned the lessons of that generation. I learned what could be effective means of presenting positions and I also observed those that weren't effective.

Those that were not effective were epitomized for Payne by animal rights activists, many of whom would not respect the opposition's opinion.

For animal rights activists, a minority group that had successfully challenged a majority view epitomized democracy. For defenders of animal research, however, this situation represented a threat to democratic principles; the animal rights movement was "imposing" its minority views on the rest of society. One side turned social unity into shame, the other turned shame into unity. The animal rights movement came to stand for all the other minority interest groups — the anti-abortion, anti-nuclear, and environmental activists — that were having a greater say in American life. This was a "textbook example," according to a pro-research *Wall Street Journal* article, of how activist groups "press their agendas" into today's political system.

> It hardly matters, for instance, that an American Medical Association poll found that 77% of adults think that using animals in medical research is necessary. Those people answered the phone and went back to their lives, working at real jobs and raising families. Meanwhile the professional activists — animal rights, anti-nukers, fringe environmentalists, Hollywood actresses, descend upon the people who create "issues" in America.
>
> They elicit sympathetic free publicity from newspapers and magazines. They do Donahue and Oprah. And they beat on the politicians and bureaucrats. They create a kind of non-stop Twilight Zone of "issues" and "concerns" that most American voters are barely aware of. They do this because it has succeeded so many times.[2]

While animal rights activists embraced an ethic of personal responsibility for animal suffering, animal researchers pinned their morality on a benevolent rendering of science. As scientists, they saw themselves fulfilling a role as nature's caretakers. This view was bolstered by environmentalism and traditional religious philosophies, as well as a conservative political agenda that led them to attack pluralism. But, like the animal rights activists, animal researchers also set themselves ideals that were difficult to realize.

Animal research is slow and incremental. Its stewardship is not instantly recognizable. At best, according to Peter Smally, a psychologist and a member of the College Town IACUC, science has made "useful, minor advances." Smally was about to retire when I interviewed him. Things that looked good twenty years ago had now faded into relative insignificance. He recalled how he had killed several monkeys in his research when he was a post-doc. The autumn sun streamed through the thin windows at the back of his office making the dust dance on a horizontal plain of light as he spoke to me. "That's the way science is," he wearily reflected.

> The studies that I did were useful, minor advances. And I'm sure that's the way most of the protocols that we're looking at are. They are minor advances. There is some pretty good stuff that comes along. But many experiments have to be done before that great breakthrough comes along. So when you look back at it thirty years later, you say, "Yeah, that looked good at the time and it was a good experiment to do then. I guess it had to be done." But I don't know.

"You see," Smally explained, leaning back in his chair and clasping his hands together behind the back of his head, "some people have the view of science that if they just do this critical experiment, then that's it, and they've discovered everything there is to know about the field. And that's not the way it is."

O'Brien believed that she was particularly vulnerable to attack for not living up to the high ideals of medical science. She knew about animal experiments going on elsewhere in the university that she felt were far more objectionable than hers. But she thought that she had been the target of threatening letters from Animals Anon because "psychologists are not perceived as saving lives." It was difficult for outsiders to appreciate her stewardship. And there was something else that made her feel even more vulnerable. There had been a rumor going around at American Psychological Association meetings that animal rights activists were attacking female researchers because they were perceived as more vulnerable to pressure than men. At Cornell University, a woman had turned back a grant because her proposed research was attacked by the animal rights activists. "I swear to God that would not have happened at institutions that were seen as being supportive of women on the faculty," O'Brien told me.

Some researchers felt vulnerable when talking about their feelings in public. Others, however, capitalized on them in a public relations campaign to defend animal research. Here the debate over animal research turned into a debate not just about feelings for animals but about the very role of feelings in public life.

Six

Learned Emotion

Animal rights supporters described their journey into animal rights activism in terms of their emotional attachments to animals. But they did not consider themselves to be emotional. Most of those I interviewed used this term to criticize others whom they believed were too angry about animal cruelty ("radicals"), too sentimental ("welfarists"), or too feminine (women). These activists favored a "rational" approach to dealing with animal cruelty. They emphasized scientific or philosophical justifications for animal protection. They advocated rights and justice for all animals, rather than compassion for pets. Why were such appeals so popular? For older activists who held professional values, being emotional made animal protection look amateurish or feminine. For the younger, idealistic activists, being emotional about pets contaminated the purity of the movement's ideology. For both groups, it trivialized animal protection.

By defining various people and situations as "emotional" or "rational," these activists attempted to construct for themselves a world in the animal rights movement that was consistent with how they wanted to live outside of it. Despite the emotional appeal of animal rights activism, this world was civil, scientific, and masculine.

Radicals

To Animals Anon, June exemplified the radical element in the animal rights movement. She had come to the College Town from the West Coast for no more serious reason than it was the landing point of a dart she had thrown at a map of North America. Once there, June drifted from job to job, working first behind the salad bar in the local cooperative and then as a hostess in a vegetarian restaurant. She was a familiar face among the health-food crowd, a free spirit, and dressed scantily in black lacy clothes. In the spring of 1991, when the engine block cracked on her pickup truck and she had to call her father for money, he gave her a lecture about "being a responsible citizen and getting a real job." She was thirty-one.

June needed that truck because she lived out in the country several miles from the College Town. Her home was a trailer with peeling wicker furniture, cardboard boxes, and pots of animal food strewn in every conceivable cubbyhole. Rabbits scurried on a rotting wooden deck, and four turkeys lived in a large wire pen in the yard. A couple of goats and a donkey would turn their great necks and meander their way through the trees toward anyone approaching the trailer. So removed was June's home from the cultivated surroundings of the College Town that, when visiting, one would feel like a World War One pilot who had accidentally landed his plane in a foreign country.

Animal rights activists called June a radical. She was more involved with the national animal rights organizations such as People for the Ethical Treatment of Animals (PETA) and Trans-Species Unlimited than small-timers like Animals Anon. Radicals were also younger than the other activists and lived alternative lifestyles — not eating or wearing any animal products. "My view of human beings," June once told me, "is that when the world was created, people were a kind of mutation. Just like a disease they took over like a cancer cell."

June cared little for family or career as long as she could keep her truck on the road and the bills paid. The walls of her home were lined with photographs of rabbits, cows, cats, and chickens, arranged like wedding pictures. "It's always possible that I will get married if I happen to fall over someone who wants to help me promote the ethical treatment of animals," June explained. Animal rights activism was, for radicals, a full-time job. Most of their friends were also in the movement. "I've devoted my life to animal rights," June told me. Her goal was to buy some land, much like the scraggy plot that she already occupied, and, with a few of her friends, set up an animal sanctuary for rescued farm animals.

Activists distinguished radicals from others in the movement most of all by their protests, which were designed to capture public attention at any expense. They paraded naked at anti-fur demonstrations. They wore cow costumes outside McDonald's. And they mocked hunters with derisive slogans and songs. Radicals did "street theater" — as they called it — because, for them, the animal rights movement lived and died by its ability to capture the media's attention. "The press has better things to do than listen to animal rights activists," June said, reflecting on the triviality that the public accords to animals. This resulted in an attitude, epitomized in various slogans, of doing "whatever it takes," and when big news breaks, like a PETA raid, to "strike while the iron is hot." What matters at the end of the day is that "you have a story." The fickle media encouraged this attitude. Activists had to compete with a chorus of other groups and events clamoring for attention. "You'll make it in the news if no one gets killed," I once heard at a meeting in the Larger City. And a Footballing Saturday in the College Town easily scuttled a funeral for animals killed by furriers.

Radicals knew that they did things in pretty poor taste. The more absurd the better. But knowing also that only a few people were prepared to stand outside Kentucky Fried Chicken on a sultry Friday night when most College Town residents were out on their decks grilling hamburgers, they rationalized that it was better to dress up as a chicken and make a jerk of yourself than to be completely ignored and have all your efforts wasted: "Bad coverage is better than no coverage."

Radicals and "Professional People Who Care About Animals"

But the older, career-oriented women in the organization disagreed. They emphasized their professional lives or their traditional conservative up-bringings in the South when talking about their animal rights activism. Linda was an attorney in the College Town. She was only a few years older than June. Before coming to Animals Anon, however, she had spent polite afternoons in "upper middle-class groups, such as church groups with a lot of southern belles, that did things the way they'd always been done." "You didn't rock the boat," Linda recalls. "You went along with the group." Animals Anon was different, since the animal rights activists were challenging her "traditional, capitalistic beliefs." These people were outspoken. They offended. They challenged the old way of doing things: the old ways of research, the old ways of being fashionable.

Linda worried that her friends would think that she was radical too. She was relieved to find that the church hall was not full of "hippies from the 1960s standing out on the street with picket signs," as she had expected of her first animal rights meeting. On the contrary, she saw an old high school friend there, whose husband was now a doctor: "somebody I could associate with in a professional sense. They were actually professional people who cared about animals, respected them." Hers was a world that required a never-ending spiral of post-graduate degrees in order to keep up, to be credible. And for Clara, another activist in the College Town, it was the opposition — the animal researchers — who exemplified the professional qualities to which she aspired. "They of course come across as the pinnacles of respectability, educated and rational people that are respected by society," she told me. "And I think that if we don't try to exude that image, then trying to get our point listened to is certainly not going to work. We need to project a professional, well-educated, rational non-emotional image in order to get our point across." Clara thought about the younger people in the group. "I guess one thing that bothers me about Animals Anon is that there's a lot of young people involved who think that the way to go is to get attention and cause a ruckus and alienate people." Indeed, June had no professional identity to preserve in the first place.

Acceptable Anger

Even the most undesirable people in an organization can serve a purpose — if only to show the rest of the members what is acceptable and what is unacceptable. Having been asked by the pastor to leave the church hall to make room for other volunteer groups, the activists were now meeting in the offices of the law firm where Linda worked. One night, an intense discussion broke out about protest strategies. Someone mentioned that a PETA member had thrown a custard pie in the face of a recently crowned "Pork Queen" in a pageant organized by promoters for the meat industry. Carol, who worried about the professional image of the organization, said that she would never have supported this. It distracted the public from learning about vegetarianism and the plight of factory-farmed pigs. Another member had written an anonymous note to the group that Saul read out at the meeting that night. "We need more thoughtful, careful education," it warned. "Stay away from publicly presenting the loony left with alienating antics and anger." Douglas disagreed. Although he was concerned about the professional image, to hide one's anger betrays the animals that suffer in silence. Flicking back his fine white hair, Douglas cleared his throat, as if he were going to give a speech. Everyone listened when this finely spoken aristocratic man spoke. "We have true education," he reminded the group, referring to animal rights literature, films, and seminars.

But every day millions of animals are dying behind
closed doors and no one raises a voice. No one is
angry. This is a betrayal to the animals. Some of us
are outraged. We must let the nation know that
some of us are outraged! We must let the nation
know that some of us are angry! People must know
that hunting is controversial. We must make people uncomfortable.

The room began to stir. Several activists broke into applause. "We need everything," Douglas continued. "Even
the civil rights activists became angry under the Black Pan-
thers. These tactics have brought us our success."

Douglas explained that he would not personally dress
up in a costume. But he would not object to others who
did. Radicals did things that the professionally minded
members, like Douglas, were not prepared to do in order
to draw the media's attention. This freed them for more
respectable activities, like giving talks at high schools and
appearing on local radio shows, and it permitted alliances
between professionals and radicals.

A few of the professionals in Animals Anon even romanticized groups like the Animal Liberation Front (ALF) —
the alleged terrorist wing of the animal rights movement.
"I'm fascinated by them," Linda said. "I think they know
what they're doing. They don't just go in and steal animals
and take them out of laboratories. They assess the situation; find out what's going on inside; try to perhaps correct
it in some other way." To activists like Linda, ALF represented a kind of ordered anarchy, an appropriate anger, a
rational response to the situation. Consequently, several

activists who objected to June's protests still wanted to be a part of ALF.

Adding to ALF's attractiveness was its exclusivity. Not just anyone could join. Many felt called, but few were chosen. Upon asking, "Who are the Animal Liberation Front?" one activist was mysteriously told by a radical, "You are." This gave ALF's radicalism a professionalism all its own, because few people knew how to go about being a part of it. It was precisely this fascination with exclusivity that led some activists to criticize another "emotional" group within the movement — the animal welfarists, exemplified by Jodie.

Animal Welfarists

For Jodie, animals were only a small part of it. Active in Parents Without Partners, Self-Help for the Hearing Impaired, the Coordinating Council for Senior Citizens, and Women in Action, Jodie could be found in many church halls. She worked as the secretary in a purchasing department at a research institute during the day but had to take up waitressing at night to raise the eight thousand dollars she needed to install a sewage system on some land that she owned. A single parent, she lived with her teenaged son, six cats, two dogs, and a couple of goldfish that she had rescued from a plastic garbage can at the state fair.

The events that Jodie organized for Animals Anon involved pets: sponsored dog washes, animal festivals, and Christmas parades with the humane society. Other activists in the College Town called these "light animal rights events," "social events," or "low-key events." They thanked

Jodie and praised her for her hard work. Yet they became impatient with her announcements, and it was often difficult to get people to sign up for her events. Why? I wondered.

Animal rights activists associated the animal welfarists like Jodie with the local humane societies. The welfarists, they believed, cared only for cats and dogs. Indeed, the humane society in the College Town held dog-training classes and helped find lost pets. They organized the Pets Are Wonderful Council to "promote the joys of pet ownership," which appeared in shopping malls on busy Saturdays with stray dogs, groomers, and veterinarians. The activists aptly called the welfarists "cat-and-dog people" or "animal lovers."

The Impurity of Animal Welfare

It is difficult to live a cruelty-free life. I met a few activists who ate meat and wore leather. They saw these as personal failings, not as contradictions to the overall animal rights philosophy. They knew, however, that skeptics would accuse them of being inconsistent. This made them feel guilty, not just for hurting animals, but for telling others not to hurt them while hurting them themselves. If you eat meat or wear leather, you keep quiet about it and make sure you do not appear on the protest lines with a hamburger or leather handbag. Most ideologies value purity.

But welfarists openly ate meat and wore animal products. They also supported some types of animal research. The shelter staff in the College Town would not sell their live animals to researchers, but they agreed to donate tissue from animals that had already been euthanized to cys-

tic fibrosis researchers at the university. The shelter manager explained that this was to "help children throughout
the world." In fact, the shelter staff sought good relations
with the public. For them, animal cruelty can be effectively
resolved by harmonizing relations between people and animals. "A lot of the people-animal problems we have can be
resolved by understanding animal behavior," the humane
educator explained to me. "We have a whole night on canine social systems," she said. "The public doesn't know
that it's normal for a dog to chew things." The shelter even
gave advice to hunters about their dogs.

Many activists criticized the shelters for relying on
"emotional appeals." The shelter was merely attempting to
please the public rather than help the animals. "They're
very caught up in what society thinks," Wendy, the preschool teacher I met at the pound seizure hearing, told
me. "They don't want to do anything to offend anyone."
Activists also used this criticism against the welfarists who
wandered into Animals Anon: "It just seems that they're
into walking dogs at a parade — fluffy-cat-and-dog walks —
rather than veal calf protests or any kind of hard-hitting
thing," June sneered.

But rejecting the welfarists presented activists with a
dilemma. It isolated them further from the public. It made
them feel extremist. Annie and Charlotte, students in the
College Town and sisters who sat together in meetings, recalled a night when Carla, a young activist, brought her husband, Rorey, to an Animals Anon meeting at the church
hall. He had carefully packed some chocolate brownies
he had made for the activists. "He was circulating them
around the room," Charlotte explained. "And somebody

asked the guy, 'Doesn't this have animal fat in it?' and the guy said, 'Well I don't know, I didn't really look.' And they said, 'You didn't read the package!' And another person said, 'Oh, I can't eat that!' — and said it loud enough that the group heard."

"They chastised him," Annie elaborated. "They chastised him in a way that was so rude that I think it just showed an element of intolerance to other people who didn't necessarily share the same living styles." Annie and Charlotte felt ashamed to be part of Animals Anon that night. The man never returned.

The Irrationality of Animal Welfare

To most activists, welfarists trivialized animal protection, not only because they pandered to the public, but also because they showed their emotional attachment to animals. Drawing on classic dichotomies between rationality and emotionality, most activists believed that their emotions alone could not justify to outsiders or themselves why they should take part in the movement. Feelings, they said, are "the fuel to" or the "passion behind" animal rights activism, but they are also "gut reactions," "impulsive," subjective, and therefore "irrational." "Your emotion comes about because of things you've learned or things you've done, the ways you react to things," Linda, the College Town attorney, told me. "That's not necessarily how the other person is going to react." Linda knew that she was likely to be dismissed by skeptics for her emotions alone. She joined Animals Anon after reading about cosmetics testing on rabbits. The rabbits reminded her of her pet beagles. It was, she said, "an emotional response." "But," she elaborated, "animal rights issues tend to be very emotional, and a lot of laws can't be changed with emotion."

> I think people can dismiss you and your statements and your actions as mere reactions. You've got to sit down and say, "We don't need this any more. This experiment is outdated." You've got to say why we don't need to treat veal calves the way we do; that we can increase spacing of the crate. We need to have more shelters. The animals are roaming the streets. Their numbers are increasing. We need to do something about it — Not, "I hate seeing an animal on the side of the road, underfed, abandoned, and so I think we should do this."

In this way, Linda searched for the facts and figures of animal cruelty: "A fact or a figure has no emotion to it. It's a statement. Something I can say, 'Well that makes sense.' Not 'I just feel that way,' but why I have that feeling."

Activists like Linda did not want to abandon their feelings altogether. Although they had always loved pets and they cried over animal rights films about cruelty, they believed that they needed intellectual justification for their feelings. Aside from statistics churned out in animal rights literature, they found this justification in some of the philosophical writings on animal rights, such as those by Tom Regan. Arnold explained:

> I use Regan's work mainly to investigate the nuts and bolts of the animal rights position as an ethical, philosophical position. My feeling is that it's simply not good enough to have a sort of inchoate, senti-

mental feeling of good will toward animals. I mean,
I think that's great. But that in itself doesn't really
justify or legitimize it on intellectual terms.

Regan's philosophy appealed to Douglas because it does
not initially talk about animals. It talks about rights.

> *The Case for Animal Rights* is a very, very scholarly,
> dispassionate, philosophical work. In some four
> hundred eighty pages he goes through the argu-
> ments of the ethics that deal with some of the rights
> philosophy. I think in the first hundred pages he
> doesn't even mention the word *animal.* He simply
> analyzes what previous philosophers have said
> about rights. The whole idea of rights has always
> fascinated me: civil rights or to what extent does
> America have the right to go into other countries.

Yet most activists accepted that animals cannot have
rights in the same way that humans can. They thought that
animals should be treated with "compassion" or "respect."
Animals are vulnerable. A more popular analogy is that
animals should be treated like children. But the philosophical discussion of rights provided them with more impersonal and therefore acceptable ways of talking about animals. Thus the animal rights movement was no longer seen
as an organization for those who loved pets or cute animals
but as an intellectual movement of justice for all animals.

This had to be made particularly clear when talking
about animal research. The popular host of a local radio
health show invited Douglas to debate animal researchers
on the air. He began by asking Douglas to summarize for

the listeners the animal rights position. Douglas cleared his throat. "Maybe the best way to explain what animal rights is, is to explain what it is *not*," he said slowly and methodically.

Many people get emotionally wrought up if they walk through the woods and they stumble on a fox or a raccoon that sits in one of those steel-jaw leg-hold traps and it's in obvious agony and pain; the steel is cutting into its flesh and it's bleeding and it's been there for many hours and you see the fear of death as you approach because it knows the trapper will come and stomp it to death. Or if they see the heart-wrenching sight of a calf that's been torn from its mother immediately after birth and shoved into one of those regulation-size crates where it spends its entire life chained by the neck and it can never move and never chew.

Now these are strong emotions. Some people cry when they see extreme acts of cruelty. And these are certainly not emotions that any one of us needs to be ashamed of. On the contrary, these are emotions that I think we ought to nurture in ourselves. But the animal rights view says: "Let us push these emotions away for just a moment and be very cool and rational about this. And if we do, we will then discover that what is wrong here is not necessarily this or that act or degree of cruelty. But what is wrong here is something much larger. What is wrong here is the entire system. A system that has put in place a good half dozen huge industries which exploit and kill vast numbers of animals, literally billions of animals in this country alone."

The animal rights philosophers have undertaken a very thorough inquiry into the ethical foundations that are involved here and have come to the conclusion that this situation and attitude is not justifiable in moral terms. And the bottom line is that what we owe the animals is not kindness and compassion but respect and justice.

And so I noticed a kind of hierarchy in the animal rights movement. The people that the activists most respected rarely talk about pets. They talk about philosophy. The philosophers themselves are the high priests of the animal rights movement. They write books. They teach at universities. Don Barnes, the animal researcher who became an animal rights activist, even went as far as to deny his affection for animals. "I'm not an animal-lover," he told a group huddled around him at a Rosenthal rally. "Some animals I like, others I don't like. To say I'm an animal-lover is the same as saying I'm a nigger lover."

Besides the philosophy, these activists sought solace from emotionalism in science itself. Saul's wife, Carol, for instance, recalled how Saul organized a candlelight vigil outside the chancellor's house at the College Town one evening, and how, instead of consulting Saul, the anchorman from the local television station approached her for a statement. The camera man and sound engineer began positioning themselves around her. "I was uncomfortable because I had never done it before — having a camera in front of me," Carol recalled. "Too many times, people say,

'I'm in the movement because I love animals,'" she told me. "I think there's more to it."

> I guess my concern is the kind of image that I want projected. For me the image needs to be people who are educated and aware and not emotional when it comes to the media. Because people who are opposed to us are very quick to jump on that. It's not emotions that change policy, that change opinions. It's being able to lay down a very logical argument for why you believe such a thing.

In front of the camera that night, she sought scientific justification for her emotions.

> Taking it from the orientation that there are alternatives, there are other ways to do it so we don't have to inflict pain on the animals. I think you have to have the emotion. But in addition you can say, "I care. But what would be a more sound type of study?" So it's sort of adding the component of justification for changing.

An understanding of science is crucial for these activists. Far from being anti-science, the activists embraced science. They read books written by medical scientists on vegetarianism. They watched science documentaries on the television. And they debated the merits of animal research in stopping cancer and AIDS. Science could be criticized only by science itself. Like the philosophers, the activists revered scientists in the movement, along with those who are well-versed in the technical aspects of medical research.

This explains why animal research often appeared to

occupy so much of the animal rights activists' attention, rather than, say, factory farming, where far more animals were killed. The media and research supporters most frequently challenged animal rights activists on their opposition to animal research, since this was where they appeared most emotional. In order to avoid looking emotional, the activists had to come up with elaborate justifications against animal research. But this only reinforced their fixation with animal research — and their anti-science image.

The Role of the Animal Welfarists

The welfarists highlighted the boundaries between being acceptably and unacceptably concerned about animals. All activists had to confront them at some point. They described themselves as having been cat-and-dog people or animal lovers before getting involved with animal rights to show how they had progressed to having more sophisticated responses toward animal cruelty. "I think you go in under emotion," Linda said. "The longer you stay in it, the more educated you become." "The emotion is still there," she added. "I don't think it subsides. But it's more a *learned emotion.*"

Women

June believed that because women are more emotional than men, they made better animal rights activists, and it made sense to have more women than men in the movement. But the professionally minded women worried that there were too many women in it. They recalled their disappointment at finding mostly housewives sitting around the tables when they arrived at the church hall for their first meeting. They worried that they would not be able to learn the rational arguments. "One thing that bothered me," Charlotte said, recalling her early meetings as we were eating breakfast with her sister at the cooperative, "was that attendance was practically all female. And some of the discussions at the meetings were real kind of emotional responses. Instead, I wanted to learn about different responses you could use — different arguments and how you respond to that. And sometimes at the meetings, they digress into these things where they say, 'Isn't that awful!' 'Isn't this horrible!' And they say, 'I can't believe that!' 'How could they do something like that?' "

If such women made the animal rights movement look emotional, then men made it look credible because men are supposed to be more rational than women. Annie and Charlotte got into their own conversation: "You start questioning," Annie said, "Why is it that more men are not coming to these meetings? And you see individual men coming, and they never come back. And you wonder why. Is it because of the way that the material is presented? Is it presented through a more emotional thing? — 'Isn't that terrible isn't that awful!' " She began to mock the women cruelly in a high-pitched voice. "I think part of it has to do with the fact that a lot of men are just brought up in a much more logical way. They like to have their rational arguments. They don't like to act totally on their fears. It just started bothering me because I thought there should be more men here because a lot of men, especially in the South, are in the leadership positions, and we should be reaching out to those people."

"I guess it's because whenever anything is given credibility, unfortunately, it is usually led by a man or a man is in the starring role," Charlotte explained. "The society listens much more to a man than they would to a woman. And I recognize that women still don't have equal status that a man has. And I guess in a way I want to take advantage of the fact that that's the way society sees it. And in order for our group to gain the credibility it needs, that is one thing we could put forward — that these issues are important to men."

Emotional Men

But the story is more complex. Animals Anon activists admired the men, even when they were emotional. Ted, Dee's husband, was a likable middle-aged man with a dimpled face and thinning hair. He wore red chunky-knit sweaters and flew planes for U.S. Air. Dee knew that he "took a lot of kidding" from the other pilots and his friends at the golf club. In fact, at work, as a joke, someone once pinned to the bulletin board a photograph of him at an anti-fur protest. Yet the animal rights activists in the Larger City couldn't get enough of Ted — even though he did all the emotional things that irritated them in a woman. He got into fights. He lost his temper. And he rarely bothered attending meetings. "I adore Ted," Wendy told me enviously.

> He's very outspoken. He's not afraid of anything or anybody. Dee tries to temper him and keep him in line, and she does a pretty good job. But he and one of our local furriers almost got into a fight in the middle of the street one time. And I couldn't

blame him. I was about ready to shake the furrier myself because he came up and attacked. He hates to just come and hear talk. He's more of a *doer*. He likes to come out and protest with us and do active things. He doesn't like to just sit and hear a bunch of talk. He's really a great guy. Dee is very lucky.

Activists praised a man's anger, but I never heard them praise a woman's. They supported street theater when Douglas supported it, but not when June supported it.

Men were praised not only for being angry. A few women admired the men in the movement because they saw them as sensitive, caring, and compassionate, even though they believed men are less emotional than women and that "emotions don't win arguments." "I can't think of any men in the movement that I don't like," Tina, one of the earliest members of the organization, explained. "They are overwhelmingly compassionate and they're feminist-oriented. It's very easy to talk to them. It's like talking to gay guys!" she laughed. "That's why women like having gay friends. The qualities that have led them into the movement is the reason I like them."

"But don't the same qualities lead women into the movement?" I asked.

"Yeah. But you don't find them as often in women. I mean I would much rather spend time with a guy — whether it's in the animal rights movement or a working relationship or in a personal relationship or whatever — who agrees with my philosophy, who is willing to talk about emotions or make himself vulnerable by being in a protest movement.

To me that's a sign of masculinity, a lack of fear to put himself out there for abuse. I think it's more admirable than Joe Blow who's out there getting drunk."

There was an economic principle at work here. The perceived scarcity of men who expressed their feelings for animals pushed up their value. Men paid their emotional dues simply in the shame they had to endure by being in an animal movement. Men's willingness to express their feelings was considered a sign of fearlessness, but in women it was a sign of weakness. Being emotional became legitimate when men did it, and women could point to men's participation in the movement to justify the legitimacy of their own feelings about animal cruelty. There was no more powerful an incentive for Shirley to quit eating meat, she told me, than when her husband — "a big strapping male, who loves his red meat" — suggested it. And a man who refused to buy his wife a fur coat was more persuasive than any anti-fur protest. "I had a law school classmate who's an SBI [State Bureau of Investigation] agent," Linda recalled. "A tough fellow, a very hard person. Used to deal in drug enforcement; solving the dregs of life, the bad scenes of addiction and killing. And that hardens you after a while." But what Linda remembers most about this man happened just after a lecture. "He pulled me aside, and he said, 'You know, I really think that it's very ugly for a woman to wear a fur coat. I would never buy my wife one and I think what you're doing is great.' " Linda paused. "He never said any more after that, and he never said it in front of anybody. But that gave me a good feeling, because I had always felt that he was a very insensitive person. A very hard person."

Men were praised for being both emotional and rational.
But women were criticized if they were not rational all of
the time.

Talkative Men

Wendy and Dee admired Ted because he was a "doer,"
not a "talker." But it appeared to me that men did most of
the talking and not much doing. Whenever there was a
debate between animal researchers and animal rights activists, men represented the animal rights position. Why
then were they praised as doers, not talkers?

The answer lies in the different situations in which men
and women talk in the animal rights movement as well as
in other public debates. Men's talk goes on in the public
sphere, in front of television cameras and radio micro-
phones, and at high schools. When Wendy said that Ted
did not like to go and just hear "talk," she meant that he
did not like to go to organizational meetings, where the
activists sorted out who was going to do what and when. But
he enjoyed the protest lines, where he got into arguments.

This was in keeping with an observation about men and
women by linguistics professor Deborah Tannen. While
issues such as abortion and animal cruelty are of interest
to large numbers of women, it is usually men that call in
to public talk shows to discuss these matters. Tannen argues that while both men and women are interested in the
topics, women do not feel as comfortable debating them in
a public forum. Although men appear not to talk at meetings, they are happy talking in public. For the same reason,
men talk when they are in the company of friends but
appear to be silent when they are at home with their wives.[1]

This explains why men are often the spokespersons for the animal rights movement, despite the fact that the movement is 80 percent female.

Does this mean that there is inequality within the animal rights movement — a movement that is supposed to advocate egalitarianism? A few women, who noticed gender inequalities where they worked, did see the situation as outright sexism. Carol called Douglas a chauvinist and said that "he would turn to a man before he'd turn to a woman to get things done." She recalled, for instance, running an information table with her husband, Saul, and a newcomer to the movement. When Saul left the newcomer's side, Douglas kept worrying that no one was helping the newcomer, even though Carol was still there. "It was as if Douglas was saying, 'Are you sure she can handle it?' — but not to my face," Carol told me. Douglas insisted, however, that he was a feminist and got upset when confronted by accusations of sexism. In fact, most activists would consider Douglas to have been helping Carol, believing that men are more comfortable doing the public talking and that they bring credibility to the animal rights movement. They want him to talk when the camera falls on them. So if Douglas was helping Carol, was it really inequality? Not in the eyes of most activists. They took advantage of men's status to bolster the status of their own cause.

The women also praised men for being the doers rather than the talkers because of the kind of talk that they associated with men. Again, Deborah Tannen argues that men talk about things that are less personal to them. They prefer to talk about world events rather than to "gossip" about interpersonal relationships. They consider this kind of "small

talk" to be trivial, whereas women use it to establish connec-
tions with one another.[2] It was not surprising, then, to find
that small talk was unwelcome at most animal rights events.
Several activists were concerned that protesters should not
socialize on the protest lines or that there should at least be
a designated "socializing zone" to control small talk. Those
who worried about the "emotional" image of the movement rarely thought of the other members of the group as
their "close friends." Socializing is considered to be a woman's activity, and it is therefore not surprising that these
activists saw it as trivial. While the men did most of the
talking at meetings and protests, their talk was never seen as
small talk or socializing.

Up until now, I have talked about men as a minority
group in the animal rights movement. But what about other
poorly represented groups? In the three years that I attended monthly animal rights meetings I only once saw an
African American at a meeting. A few activists wished that
there were more in the movement. African Americans, they
believed, would help legitimate the movement because
their presence would show that animal rights activism has
broad appeal. "I don't want it to be looked at as a white
middle-class movement," Wendy once told me. Moreover,
as an oppressed minority, African Americans could speak
from direct experience about discrimination. Activists drew
strong parallels between the civil rights movement and the
animal rights movement.

At the same time, activists were not surprised that African Americans did not attend the meetings. They were, the
activists rationalized, still concerned with protecting their
own rights and did not, in Douglas's words, "have the lux-

ury" to take part. But this rationalization was tricky. African Americans, Douglas pointed out, might have taken offense at being compared with animals. And activists had no more reason to assume that African Americans did not care much about animals than to assume that they did.

I am guilty of making such assumptions too. Because I only once saw an African American in the movement, I assumed that she was atypical and I did not think it was worth my while to interview her. Consequently, I learned little about what she did or did not get out of the movement. Maybe this is why we have far more accounts of white middle-class attachments to animals and tend to ignore other groups. We frequently fail to recognize the emotions of those we do not know or understand.

Those who derisively called others "emotional" in Animals Anon were usually those who felt the most vulnerable about being discredited outside the movement for the same reason. Professionals who defined their worlds in terms of hard-earned educational qualifications and careers were the most concerned about not being seen as emotional and not being tainted by the organization's leftist hippie image. They had to fight this image to get where they were in their careers. The activists in the Larger City chapter, which had fewer such professionals than the one in the College Town, worried less about their emotional image. It was an altogether more relaxed organization — resembling any other civic group with its yard sales, pot-luck dinners, social gatherings, and cozy friendships.

The animal rights movement has traditionally been a women's movement that has fought to infuse feelings into a male-dominated, competitive society. Indeed, recent feminists have tried to show how women are more concerned than men about relationships, responsibility, and care. And the ecofeminists say that this ethic should complement animal rights activism. But how do women really perceive this way of looking at the world? How does this academic discourse about women as nurturers enter into their everyday lives and situations?

Where women are trying to enter what they see as a man's world, talk of care and responsibility appears to hold little legitimacy. Recall the art students that Belenky and her colleagues studied who wanted to intellectualize art rather than enjoy its beauty. Such women moved from basing their opinions about art on their feelings to basing them on objective procedures and rules. They became "especially suspicious of ideas that feel right." They sought the truth "by suppressing the self, taking as impersonal a stance as possible toward the object so that the flower of reason may flourish."[3]

In the same way, many of the women in Animals Anon denigrated their feelings about animal cruelty as impulsive, irrational, and subjective. They criticized those who love pets. They put animals in the impersonal category of sentient beings, a culture unto itself. Moral authority rests on substantiating feelings about animal cruelty with scientific, rational, or intellectual arguments. Once famous for criticizing the male-dominated medical profession for lack of compassion, today's animal rights activists embrace emotional neutrality, science, and ways of looking at the world that they consider masculine.

A few activists recognized this contradiction. Being

emotional about animals encourages outsiders to dismiss the movement as trivial. But if one trivializes one's emotions, then one trivializes one's own reasons for becoming an animal rights activist. "It's a shame," Annie said, "because I think being emotional has as much credit as somebody who comes to it rationally, you know." "And that's what we hope to accomplish," Charlotte added. "That sort of balance between rationality and emotions. It would be great if we didn't have to end up going one way or the other." To the extent that activists used the rational approach as a response to their emotions, it was still their emotions that led them to their moral outlook.

Seven

Television Doctors

S ome animal researchers and technicians have been
reluctant to speak out against the animal rights movement. To avoid being targeted or publicly shamed,
they have "gone into the closet"[1] with animal research. In
the College Town and the Larger City, however, as in other
parts of the United States, other researchers pursued a
different strategy. They joined forces with the National Association for Biomedical Research (NABR) and the Coalition for Animals and Animal Research (CFAAR) to
counter what they perceived as a growing threat to animal
research from animal rights activists.

In their interviews with me, researchers justified their
work by pointing to their achievements in their specialized
fields and to their personal codes of conduct in animal
experiments. But in pro-research campaigns, researchers
had to translate these sentiments into more tangible benefits for public consumption. In a carnival of yellow and
white awnings, "Truth Tables," cookies and coffee, and
speeches and clapping, university administrators, animal
researchers, physicians, surgeons, and representatives from
patient groups gathered to testify against the animal rights

155

activists at conferences and symposia. At virtual pep rallies for science, they sought to provide "public education" and to "get the facts straight about animal research."

Researchers believed they had to do more than talk about the scientific merits of animal research. Unlike the animal rights activists, they believed that only by showing their emotions could they reach the public. Researchers took this challenge seriously. In a letter printed in *Science* and distributed to College Town researchers, scientists who formed a pro-research organization in California noted: "We have learned that when we are dealing with the activists and with the public, the most effective approach is not only to use rational dialogue, but also to make the topic emotionally appealing."[2] In this vein, researchers in the College Town and the Larger City attempted to win support from the pubic by portraying scientists as heroic, compassionate, and victimized.

Heroic Scientists

The painstaking and incremental process of animal research has to be accelerated into stark medical triumphs in pro-research presentations to the public. "Think of it as an inverted pyramid," explained a smartly dressed public relations woman at a workshop for media novices. "Do not present all your data first, then write your conclusion. Lead with your conclusion. Then if time allows, follow up with your explanation." Physicians and surgeons are particularly relied upon to do this, since they deal with the everyday applications of animal research. "We have forgotten," a surgeon introduced as Don Keating kept repeating in an evangelical tone at the Symposium for Animal Research in the Larger City.

> We have forgotten that people in our grandparents' generation frequently died from complications of appendicitis and communicably acquired pneumonias. We do not appreciate how far we have advanced in the last century, and how important animal models have been in achieving these advances. Who among us has ever seen anybody die of whooping cough, measles, or polio? We take for granted these vaccines that were developed with animals, and that have enabled these life-threatening diseases to be brought under control. Most current practicing physicians don't know how lethal common bacterial infections were prior to the advent of penicillin and the many generations of antibiotics that have since been developed and tested in animals before being administered to humans.

This state of collective amnesia means having to remind the public that there is, in fact, much to celebrate about modern medical achievements. Speakers at the symposium in the Larger City presented a history of animal-based medical research that focused on "breakthroughs" and "quantum leaps" in the development of cures for "one-time scourges" in order to infuse the story of animal research with inspiration and awe. It is necessary, as Keating said, to "put things in perspective" in a society that is "losing track" of its achievements. Past-present comparisons are needed to highlight the triumphs of medical research and remind the public that humanity has, indeed, something to be proud of. "We don't even think twice when kids have measles," Keating continued.

> Very rarely do they get it any more. Small pox was endemic in the country fifty years ago. It doesn't exist on the planet earth anymore. And polio, the same way. We've lost track of our perspective. We don't take things and put them in their proper perspective anymore. I've see wards of patients dying of tuberculosis. I'm talking about this decade. All these problems we don't have anymore in America.

The triumphs of animal research can be further appreciated by comparing our own society with those that do not have modern medicine. Third World countries, Keating pointed out, provide a glimpse into the past before biomedical research. He recalled for the audience his missionary work in Africa, where he witnessed "flocks of children dying every day from measles." Another surgeon described a time when the Romans banned autopsies on humans as "a Dark Age in medical progress."

It was not just the history of medical science that pro-research speakers used to exalt animal research but also its future, brimming with promise and hope, always "on the brink of" more breakthroughs. "I hope that the future will be as staggeringly different from the present as our past is different from the present," said Keating in closing.

> It could be, and we must not let it fall short of this goal. It could be fifty years from now or twenty-five years from now that there will be another surgeon standing here who will be able to say: "I have ac-

tually witnessed patients with AIDS," and, "I have actually witnessed patients with cystic fibrosis." In awe, people would say to him, "You're kidding!" Wouldn't that be fabulous?

Accounts of the triumphs of medical science often turn to laudatory anecdotes about the researchers themselves. Researchers rely on patients, billed as the beneficiaries of animal research, to express their gratitude for contributions to medical science. Glen Alder represented the most vocal of these in "Perspectives on Animal Research," a symposium that the Association for Biomedical Research organized in the College Town. Over a hundred people filled a lecture theater, most of whom were graduate students and faculty from the university. The symposium began with a presentation about the animal rights movement and speeches about the achievements of animal research. Then Alder came to the podium. A tall man with pointed features, he began telling his story to a gripped audience. In 1971, Alder explained, he had been a gold miner in southern Arizona when, at nineteen years old, he was almost killed in a fiery plane crash that left half his body burned. With his skin like molten plastic, he spent ten weeks in traction recovering from a compound fracture in his leg that he had also sustained in the accident. One night, as Alder was recuperating, his friend Clinton Wilde called him on a ham radio and started complaining to him about "a bunch of crazies" who were protesting the use of lab animals at the University of Arizona. Wilde suffered from multiple sclerosis and was volunteering in an experimental drug treatment program. The drugs that he was taking had been developed in animal experiments. In appreciation, he had founded an organization for incurably ill patients to support animal research.

After talking with Wilde, Alder reflected on his own lucky escape, his countless skin grafts, pain killers, and antibiotics that had all been developed on animals. He read more about animal research and the animal rights movement. He studied speeches by Ingrid Newkirk and the movement's publicity and fund-raising campaigns. He began to travel around the country giving talks about his experiences with medical science. Medical researchers became his friends. "I know how emotionally devastating it can be," he told the audience at the College Town that night, "to be a scientist who has dedicated his or her life to helping others through the advancement of medical knowledge, and to have your labs vandalized by animal rights terrorists or receive hate mail and death threats every day." Most of all, Alder expressed his gratitude to the medical researchers, something he was reminded of every time he stood up or walked. "Yes, the benefits of animal research are very real," he told the audience, his voice becoming solemn.

And to some of us they are evident every day. And we're grateful to them. We're grateful for the research that's been done in the past that has helped us. We're grateful for the researchers and the rest of the research team that has made all of this possible. And I know that we have some members of the research community with us here in the audience tonight. And I'd like to take this opportunity to say thank you for myself personally, and for the rest of our members. 'Cause I think that's something that's not been said up until now.

In New England, Arnold Arluke observed in a study of the animal research community, patients went further than merely saying thank you. They formed an entire organization that was literally called "Thank You Researchers." Its participants not only thanked researchers but, with religious zeal, positively deified them. "I have been blessed by every member of this room," one former patient said, during a seminar.

I had primary biliary disease. I was told I would die in two years, but I'm still here. You are looking at a genuine miracle. But miracles don't happen. That's what science and medicine are all about — to discover wondrous miracles. I'm grateful, thankful and indebted to all of you. Thank you, thank you, thank you. And thank you on behalf of the millions of people that depend upon your skill. I am here, alive and well, because I have benefited from scientific investigation using animals. I watched my son graduate from Law School. I celebrated my thirty-fifth anniversary. Ten years ago I lay comatose and dying. My family was told to plan my obituary. The liver transplant saved my life. I am alive and well. How can I describe what it feels like to be reborn? How can I explain how grateful I am to you for each new day?[3]

It was not only patients who hinted at the divine source of medical knowledge. "I really feel that knowledge is a blessing," a veterinarian studying Tay Sachs disease in cats says in a brochure put out by the local affiliate of the NABR in the College Town. "My idea of Heaven is knowing absolutely everything."

The Compassionate Scientist

To reach the public, the NABR encourages scientists to present themselves in a personal and egalitarian manner rather than with the affective neutrality that scientists are supposed to show toward their clients. This often means that researchers play down their professional roles as research scientists and try to appear more like caring family physicians. Pro-research journalist Katie McCabe warned scientists in a speech before the California affiliate of the NABR:

> If you can't humanize your story, reporters won't write it and editors won't buy it. Know that this is not a clean, fair fight. Those who go in expecting reasonable debate will lose out to shrill, emotional arguments and ad hominem attacks. Yes, you must address the animal activists' arguments about alternatives, duplication, et cetera, but you will only win by humanizing your view point — by being a human first concerned about other human beings. Be a human being first, a scientist second.[4]

To help them appear more "human," researchers were encouraged to tell personal stories that afforded glimpses into their inner-most feelings. "As uncomfortable as this makes you feel as scientists," McCabe argued, "I believe people's hearts must be won until they listen to the substance of your arguments." Of one exemplary researcher, who introduced her to patients with Parkinson's disease, McCabe noted: "Suddenly the issue of animal research became very personal. I had what every reporter wants: a people story. The human element was critical; the scientist became the man next door, a man who admitted to conflicted feelings about animal research but who had chosen to continue doing it because of the human benefits." Accordingly, color pictures in glossy brochures depict white-coated researchers bent over children. In "The Compassionate Quest," a heart surgeon keeps photographs of children on his desk. "When one of my patients dies," he is quoted as saying, "all I can do sometimes is come back to my office and cry. That's where the issue of animal studies gets very clear for me. I don't like to see an animal die. But I *hate* to see a child die." "Time for Charlotte," one of the most lavish accounts distributed in pro-research literature, tells the story of a little girl born with a congenital heart and lung defect. Her doctors are in a "race against time" to perfect the surgical techniques necessary to save her by practicing on lambs. But animal rights activists are "threatening to steal much of the time" from the doctors by "invading research facilities and filing ridiculous lawsuits."

In pro-research presentations, animals, like children, become the objects of compassion. An American Medical Association resource kit reminds readers: "Scientists aren't white-coated Frankensteins. They are literally the people next door. They have families and pets. They have sons who love their dogs, and 12-year-old daughters who are crazy about horses. Their compassion is the first line of defense against cruelty."[5] In fact, pets—the animals that animal rights activists feel acutely embarrassed to talk about with the media—receive the most attention in pro-research campaigns. At the county commissioners' hearing on pound seizure, research defenders agreed with the animal rights activists that many animals die in pounds because of human irresponsibility. Yet they argued that the animals' lives are further wasted if they are not used in experiments. To use them in research is a way to honor them in the face of the community's irresponsibility. Most animal researchers announced with pride that they were "animal welfarists"—a label that animal rights activists are ashamed of.

Researchers' commitment to animal welfare went beyond words. At the county commissioners' hearing, the chair of the biology department in the Larger City university offered to donate one thousand dollars for electronic name tags that would help pounds identify missing pets and prevent them from accidentally ending up in the labs as research subjects. Researchers showed their compassion for laboratory animals too. "Who Cares About Laboratory Animals?" one pamphlet reads, outlining laboratory animal care procedures. At the Symposium for Animal Research in the Larger City, laboratory animals, like the researchers, became the heroes of medical progress. "We owe a great deal to these animals for helping all of us," a senior administrator announced in an opening speech. Later in the symposium, Gabe Johnson declared the animals "partners in research" and called for a round of applause.

I close with a word of thanks to those dogs who provided what was necessary for my eighty-nine-year-
old mother to have both her hip joints replaced.
From a life of incredible pain, being confined
to life in a wheel chair, she now spends about six
hours a day doing adult literacy education.

In showing their concern for animals, pro-researchers
thought it important to point out that animal research
benefited them too. "With cancer," the community veterinarian Sam Harvey explained to the county commissioners, "research helps animals and man." Vaccines for
rabies, distemper, feline leukemia, and canine parvovirus,
he pointed out, were all tested on animals. Researchers
emphasized that it is disease, not researchers, that kills
animals. "No one sets out to kill an animal," the dean of a
local medical school said. "Animals accidentally die in the
search for a cure." And in one of the most popular pro-
research posters, the "real killers" are virulent diseases pic-
tured in color on microscope slides. "If we stop animal
research," the poster asks, "who'll stop the real killers?"

The Victimized Scientist

The portrayal of scientists as heroes in the College Town
and Larger City symposia could be made all the more com-
pelling with descriptions of their apparent victimization
by animal rights activists. Here, research supporters presented their own stories of betrayal — the betrayal of animal researchers. Through puritanical dedication, they had

given of themselves to humanity. "These scientists are high-minded individuals who forgo the rich rewards of medical practice and pass their new insights readily on to their clinical colleagues," declares a physiologist in a 1984 issue of the *Buffalo Physician*.[6] In return, the animal rights movement has framed these should-be heroes as "the enemy."[7] An Americans for Medical Progress brochure shows a man's hands lashed together at the wrists by a rope, with the bold-print caption, "What Are We Doing to Our Research Scientists?" A *Reader's Digest* article reproduced and widely distributed by the NABR describes the animal rights movement as "arresting the progress of science," creating a "regulatory straitjacket," "shackled experiments," and "damaging setbacks";[8] another article from the same magazine announces the "animal rights War on Medicine."[9]

In print and other media, research supporters focus on the activists' "terrorist" escapades. The Animal Liberation Front (ALF) is, according to an article in *Physician's Management*, "on the same list [in Scotland Yard] as the Irish Republican Army, the Palestine Liberation Organization and the Black September Movement."[10] In a video made by a television company in San Francisco and shown at a training workshop at the institute in the park, reporters describe the animal rights movement as "a group gone violent." In one scene, heavy plumes of black smoke fill the sky—apparently a London fur-retailing store that animal rights activists had attacked and set fire to. Journalists interview a gangly ALF member in what they describe as "a seedy hotel." His face is masked with a black stocking and his voice eerily disguised. This film, the workshop speaker told the trainee researchers, "adequately reflects the kind of environment in which we find ourselves using animals in research today." Gabe Johnson, the College Town pediatrician, even suggested that the Department of Defense should take over animal research.

Shared experiences of contacts with the animal rights movement confirmed the activists' terrorist image promoted by the NABR. Activists seemed to live like terrorists; "the shambles of the apartment that was his home," Rosenthal described one activist's residence where police discovered a hit list of animal researchers. An "unmarked warehouse, tucked between an auto-parts store and a plumbing contractor is the headquarters of People for the Ethical Treatment of Animals — the country's largest animal-rights group," according to an article by Katie McCabe.[11] Animal rights activists even look like terrorists. Rosenthal recalled her first encounter with the movement. In a public hearing, she had persuaded the shelter board to sell animals to research. After the meeting, a slender, hollow-eyed person, with a few days' growth of beard approached her. "Kinda looked like Yasir Arafat," Rosenthal commented. The stranger told Rosenthal that he belonged to an organization that breaks into labs and destroys equipment. "You're on our list," the man said. Rosenthal asked for his name. "Well, you can understand that under the circumstances, I prefer to be known as Saint Francis," he replied mysteriously and left.

Stories of animal rights terrorism intertwine with those of researchers' family lives such that the images of the compassionate and victimized researcher reinforce one another. Rosenthal thus marks the events of the controversy surrounding her research with events in her domestic life.

She recalls the day she came to speak at the animal shelter because it was her daughter's first birthday. She told of researchers who had to provide police surveillance to protect their children. And she recalled a letter from an anonymous animal rights activist saying, "We're going to take your husband and screw his head into the floor with a big screw because he deserves that." Indeed, as with the animal rights activists, research defenders worried that children were particularly vulnerable to the dangers inspired by the opposition. Children, they feared, would be discouraged from becoming scientists,[12] or they will be morally polluted by learning the animal rights activists' violent ways. People for the Ethical Treatment of Animals (PETA), according to Alder, started a campaign directed at children — "PETA Kids." A story appeared in one of its publications about an eleven-year-old boy who had taken some glass orbs from the Christmas tree against his mother's wishes. He put them in his backpack and bicycled to the nearest hardware store, where he purchased some red paint. Outside the shop, he filled the orbs with paint and sealed them with wax. On his bike again, he headed for a Burger King restaurant and flung the paint-filled orbs at the large glass windows, which cracked and dripped with the fake blood. "Attacking private property," Alder chastised, "is not a good way to educate children. I think it doesn't speak well for any organization to portray someone who defaced private property like that as being a hero figure for other children to look up to."

But in their presentations and their conversations with me, pro-researchers could not point to any specific acts of terrorism undertaken by the local activists. Instead, they accused them of another kind of violence: deception and insidiousness. Activists, they said, are liars. They stage photographs of animal cruelty and misquote animal researchers. Worse still, they are masking a "radical" agenda of abolishing all animal research under the moderate façade of animal welfare organizations—an iron fist in a velvet glove. They are "infiltrating" the private areas of society: humane organizations, schools, and even homes. "The animal rights movement has worked its way into our living rooms without us even realizing that it was a possibility," an angry woman in the audience at the College Town symposium observed. Alder agreed. PETA's name, he pointed out, has appeared on movie stars' T-shirts in television shows, giving subliminal messages to their audiences. This situation was even more worrying than violent attacks on individual scientists because the victims are society at large.

Some of the scientists I interviewed found solace in the message of pro-research organizations. Beth, a young graduate student, described her local CFAAR chapter as a "support group." "Before we formed, there was really no group on campus that was pro-research," she told me. "We assume that most of the scientific community is pro-research, but they don't have any formal group to say they are." The pro-research organizations allowed such researchers to turn their shame into pride in a community in which animal rights activists had deprived them of it.

But pro-research organizations presented scientists with new dilemmas. The more one drew attention to animal rights activists' campaigns, the more one inadvertently substantiated them. Rosenthal complained that the animal rights activists had disrupted research, ushered in a new regulatory era, and diverted money away from medical research into protecting researchers from terrorism. But when I wrote these things in a grant proposal, she said that I was biased against the researchers for overstating the impact of the animal rights movement on animal research. I was giving them too much credit.

Pro-research campaigns did not appeal to everyone. One physician refused to display Rosenthal's pro-research literature because, he said, his staff were sympathetic to the animal rights movement and might be upset by it. Others intimately involved with animal research also distanced themselves from the NABR. George Cramer, the veterinarian in the College Town university, learned early on that he was unsuited to its slick presentations. Approaching sixty, with a pink face and a receding hairline that he often joked about, Cramer was invited by pro-research organizers to attend a workshop on talking to the media about animal research. Not knowing what to expect, he came in his regular work clothes, which were usually hidden under his white coat. The speaker scolded him. She did not like his tie. He had apparently mixed his colors badly for the camera. She used him as an example to the others. "One of the worst things you can do," she told the participants, "is put some middle-aged guy in a white coat who's balding in front of the animal rights activists to be the institutional representative." It was as if research supporters were trying to promote a television image of doctors in which medical authority rested on appearance, as in the advertisement for aspirin in which an actor proclaims, "I'm not a doctor, but I play one on TV." The movie star Charlton Heston even appeared on a pro-research pamphlet. It was this appearance-based authority and lay rendering of science that researchers like Cramer objected to in the animal rights movement.

Indeed, scientists have traditionally distinguished themselves from the rest of society by embracing emotional neutrality, natural explanations, and technical qualifications.[13] But in pro-research campaigns, animal research takes on a supernatural quality — miraculous and unexplainable for media consumption. Often posed as the enemy of science, God now joins the side of scientists and legitimates them. Rather than calling on experts, animal research supporters call on patients, practitioners, families, and even animals to testify on behalf of science. If scientists are influenced by their intuition, emotions, and values, then what distinguishes them from the animal rights activists?

But then again, the world of animal research shows how arbitrary traditional dichotomies between emotions and rationality, religion and science can be. These scientists weave a sense of the spiritual and emotional into their work. Through their religious and emotional appeals, research supporters are still reproducing much of the culture and ideology of science. Their emotions center on achievement — achievement over ascription, paternalism over equality, order over disorder, control over autonomy. Whereas the animal rights activists I spoke with emphasized the inherent good qualities of animals over people, the pro-researchers emphasized the achievements of people over animals. "Show me a rat that has written a symphony or a novel that lasted for two hundred years," Alder challenged me.

Eight

Regulations

Bureaucracy, the 1930s social critic Karl Mannheim said, turns policy decisions into administrative problems. It turns ethics into procedures, moral quandaries into codifications. What does not fit into preconceived cognitive frameworks are bracketed and discarded. Bureaucrats thus avoid conflict. One administrator's problem becomes another's job.[1] The bureaucratization of laboratory animal welfare that began after the Animal Welfare Act of 1966 has been another response to the animal research controversy.

This bureaucracy was particularly elaborate at the College Town university, which encompassed many departments and a medical school. At the top, senior research administrators — vice chancellors and deans — peered down long chains of authority that took them far from the animal holding facilities to carpeted offices with latticed windows in the colonial-style administrative buildings. They oversaw middle-level administrators: the veterinarian and the Institutional Animal Care and Use Committee (IACUC). These, in turn, oversaw principal investigators, namely, research scientists at various stages in their careers — some clambering for tenure, others established as full professors — consultants, and research physicians. At the bottom was a relative underclasss of animal caretakers, technicians, and graduate assistants.

The regulations surrounding animal welfare, according to senior administrators, are supposed to provide a rational consensus over which experiments are legitimate. They attempt to distill moral dilemmas surrounding animal research into procedures that, if followed correctly, will amount to the ethical treatment of animals: Were the experiments "rational" (the term researchers use to describe useful experiments)? Were alternatives considered? Were anesthetics used? Were the animals housed in clean environments? "There's no morality involved," David Nathan once said. "It's a procedural kind of thing."

The regulations are supposed to be beyond personal opinions and emotions. As Mable Payne, the university's legal councilor put it, "The law codifies a minimum consensus about ethical or moral behavior. Anything beyond that is your own personal choice, your own personal morality." Indeed, senior administrators like Payne were able to separate their personal opinions from their institutional roles. "I don't have the luxury as a lawyer to take a confessional approach; whether or not I agree with animal research," she told me when I pushed her for her own opinions in the controversy. "My involvement over the years has been to ensure that we meet with the Department of Agriculture's guidelines about the use of animals in research." But this separation could not be made by those who dealt with the day-to-day enforcement of the regulations — the IACUC and the university veterinarian. Their decisions were influenced much more by their relationships with animals, animal caretakers and technicians, and principal investigators than by formal regulations.

Relationships with Animals

A complex web of regulatory bodies, each with its own inspectors and guidelines, oversees the nation's laboratory animals. In addition, each institution may have its own handbook of procedures and informal codes. The result is a myriad of regulations and guidelines surrounding laboratory animal care. Every six months, IACUC members tour the animal holding facilities looking for violations. They spend most of their time dealing with regulations about keeping the animals and the facilities clean. Even an unpleasant smell hints at broader problems: there are too many animals, ventilation is inadequate, or cages have not been cleaned. The committee must consider health hazards that newcomers to research might never think about. Cracked floor tiles allow dirt to accumulate in the jagged crevices. Giant stainless-steel industrial cage-washers that fail to operate at the correct temperature do not sterilize equipment properly. And a sack of food left propped up against a wall attracts vermin.

But animals sometimes thrive in conditions that the regulations are designed to prevent. The "Bat Tower" provides one of the most colorful examples of this. A researcher in the College Town was studying the echolocation of bats. Committee members knew him to be one of the leading authorities on the topic. He kept his bats in an old cooler, the closest thing he could find to a cave. Admittedly the place was full of excrement, and the researcher himself even joked about having to wear a gas mask whenever he entered. But the bats apparently thrived in these conditions. "If ever you've been in a bat cave, that's the way bats like to live," he pleaded with the committee. "Apparently there's something about having the feces all over that makes the bats happy. As silly as it sounds, if I clean it up, I assure you that you will have dead bats." While this example represents an extreme case, several committee members agreed that the facilities that appear to be the most natural for the animals are those that violate the most regulations. There was one facility in the College Town, for instance, where researchers kept dogs for blood samples. It was a mile away from the university on a hill near an artificial lake. The buildings were older than those of the other facilities—large and shoddy, with high ceilings and enormous glass windows. The animal caretakers kept the dogs in semi-outdoor pens with a big fan for cooling, unlike the artificially air-conditioned dungeons of the other facilities. There was something cheerful about the place. Even the lobby was bright with sunlight. The dogs, barking and greeting the committee with wagging tails, seemed more contented here than elsewhere. But George Cramer, the veterinarian at the College Town university, called the facilities "marginal," and the immunologist Henry Weiss described them as "eighth-rate." "They're good for the animals but not in terms of the regulations," he said.

Sometimes, the committee had to enforce regulations that made conditions worse for the animals. Cramer built a larger pig pen to meet requirements of the American Association for Accreditation of Laboratory Animal Care, a prestigious accreditation board. When the U.S. Department of Agriculture (USDA) inspectors came with their notepads and checklists, they told him that his pens were still too small according to National Institutes of Health (NIH) regulations. Pigs must be able to turn 360 degrees without touching the sides of an enclosure. Cramer knew, however, that if you put five pigs in one-hundred-square-foot pen, they all like to crowd into one corner and roll on top of one another. But to comply with the regulations, Cramer had to house some of the pigs in an outdoor facility, where they needed constant sprays of water to keep them cool. The sprays turned their excreta into muddy rivers in which the pigs would wallow in the heat. "The pigs stayed covered in mud, living in filth," Cramer told me. "And that was better from the standpoint of the Department of Agriculture's interpretation of the law, than my professional judgment."

When there was less oversight, the committee ignored regulations rather than make conditions worse for the animals. This is what happened with the College Town cats. Pediatricians at the College Town university used cats to teach emergency workers how to pass tubes down a child's throat. Cats, like children, are difficult to intubate because of the truncated shape of their windpipes. Students can learn how to manipulate the tube by practicing on cats. Because the NIH guidelines discourage researchers from repeatedly operating on the same animal, the cats should have been killed after each demonstration. In the College Town, however, instructors were using the same cats every time they taught intubation. Weiss, an outspoken member of the committee, vehemently challenged the chair about using the cats repeatedly. He had a special affection for cats and suspected that the university was trying to save money rather than look after the animals.

Dwayne Spalding, the chair of the committee, tried to assure Weiss that the cats did not mind the repeated surgery. In fact, they enjoyed being handled by the staff. New cats, he argued, would experience greater stress than the ones they were using already. Weiss was skeptical. He knew that Spalding was a strong advocate of using animals in teaching, and so he went to see the cats for himself. Sure enough, he later admitted, he had never seen such placid cats. They hopped up to him and started purring as soon as he approached the cage. Weiss relented. "While, in general, repeat procedures are really not a good idea, oddly it didn't seem to harm the cats. So my opinion was to reuse them."

Researchers not only ignored regulations they felt were impractical but they ignored those that contradicted their emotional attachments to the animals. Researchers who worked with larger animals for long periods, especially with cats and dogs, became so attached to them that when the experiments ended, they could not bear to euthanize them. "The investigator comes and plays with them every once in a while, but he can't bring himself to have the dogs killed," Weiss explained. "The investigators are sometimes very smart. They say they are using them again and again, but they may just come and use them as a source of blood." Admittedly, such emotions once led Weiss himself to violate NIH guidelines. The guidelines prohibit researchers from taking research animals out of the laboratory. Regulators fear that the animals might be abused by outsiders, or that they might carry dangerous diseases or toxins. This means that all animals must be killed after researchers use them in experiments. But Weiss recalled a time when, as a junior faculty member, he was testing immunizations on a goat and the experiments were coming to an end. The goat had grown too large for the enclosure and the veterinarian said that it was cruel to keep it for much longer. "Bleed him, and we'll kill him," he told Weiss. "No, I need the goat," Weiss pleaded — though he had already collected all the blood samples he needed and still had a whole freezer full of it. The truth was that Weiss had become attached to the goat. "I didn't want to kill the goat," he told me, "because it was a nice goat and I kinda liked it. Goats happen to be very likable animals. They don't smell so good if they're males, but they're very nice animals. They're sort of like cats — the bovine animals — and I enjoy them. And this was a very nice goat. I trained it! I could manipulate the goat without any restraint." Weiss began to try to negotiate with the vet to keep the goat but the vet was reluctant. "You immunized the goat, and what would happen if someone had a goat barbecue and ate the goat?" the vet told him, worrying about the substances that Weiss had injected into it. "Look, I'm not going to let you kill the goat," Weiss insisted. "I'll swear I need it for experiments, but you ain't gonna kill that goat." "What was decided," Weiss recalled, "was that at a certain time, when nobody would be around the animal facility, a certain truck would drive up to that animal facility, and if the goat kinda disappeared, they would just assume that the goat must somehow or other have died and somebody had forgotten to do something with it." In collusion with the vet, Weiss arranged for the goat to be shipped out to a remote farm belonging to one of his friends, where it lived for ten years.

One experiment triggered such powerful emotions that committee members did not want to approve it, even though according to regulations it was useful and humane. A researcher wanted to develop protective boiler suits for men who worked on high-voltage electric cables. Occasionally these men had been known to slip and receive deadly shocks. There was talk in the protocol of shaving rats' fur, putting them in a chamber, and burning them with high-voltage shocks. The committee fell silent after the chair read the details at the monthly meeting. "There's the emotional thing to it," Peter Smally, a committee member recalled. "It's one thing to do surgery on anesthetized animals. It's another thing to take a rat — even though it's anesthetized — and put him into this furnace and zap-zap him with this high-voltage stuff. It's just the empathy with the animal, I suppose. How would you like to be put in there? I mean, I know it sounds almost irrational." Weiss agreed. "I have to admit, there are very few things that really go against the grain. But this is one where I think under any circumstances I would have trouble, deep down, approving. I know the investigator is an expert. But I guess that we all have things that really kind of go against the grain." Weiss and Smally were relieved when the researcher decided to undertake his experiments at another institution.

The committee also had to consider the public's emotions about animals. Most of the members agreed that they spent more time reviewing proposals to use cats, dogs, and baby rats in experiments than they did reviewing proposals to use other animals. These experiments, they thought, were likely to be controversial with the public. All animals are supposed to receive equal treatment under the law and the committee was not supposed to be influenced by public opinion. But when cats, dogs, and baby rats were used, the committee would try hard to find ways to justify or criticize the research from a scientific perspective or from the point of view of the regulations. This way, it would not look as if their decision had been based on emotion or political expedience.

Where emotions prevailed, then, the committee clung to the regulations to justify their decisions. But the opposite could also happen. Where regulations prevailed, committee members clung to their emotions. In distinguishing themselves from other university committees, IACUC members emphasized that they were not a rubber stamp. This distinguishing feature manifest itself in brainstorming sessions during the meetings, in which the chair would ask members to express their anxieties, no matter how unscientific. One young committee member told me:

> The chair lets everyone say exactly what is on their minds. And I think that for this kind of committee, that approach is entirely appropriate. Some of the discussions we get into are at an emotional level. There is something about a particular protocol that you don't like and you can't quantify it. You can't necessarily put your finger on exactly what it is that's wrong, but something just doesn't feel right. I think there are many people in a university setting who wouldn't want to hear that kind of thing.

Relationships with Animal Caretakers, Technicians, and Research Assistants

Animal caretakers, technicians ("techs"), and graduate assistants look after animals and carry out routine research surgery. They are directly under the control of the veterinarians. The animal caretakers and techs that I spent time with were different from the other people I met in the world of animal research. I enjoyed their meetings enormously. There was always joking and exchanging of personal stories. Cramer, who ran the meetings, would join in. In the space of one morning, I heard that one staff member had had a miscarriage, another was pregnant, and Cramer was going deaf and couldn't hear high-pitched noises. This was an advantage, he admitted, when his wife was in a temper, because he couldn't hear her. Everyone laughed.

Caretakers and techs differed from other research personnel in another way. Half of those who attended meetings were African Americans. From the mandatory advertisements for positions, I knew their salaries to be not much more than my graduate stipend. Stanley, the animal rights activist who used to be an animal technician, once told me that he became a tech not out of any grand ideals about science but because he "needed a job at the time." Indeed, the animal caretakers and techs did the dirtiest and most routine tasks: One woman described being covered in urine while clipping a monkey's toenails. Another told of how a researcher left his "sharps" (syringes) lying around in her office — sharps that he was responsible for disposing of. Caretakers worked night shifts, cleaned cages, and shoveled shit.

"Animal welfare is everyone's responsibility" was a slo-
gan that I heard often in workshops and demonstrations
for research personnel on laboratory animal care. Yet everyone's responsibility could easily become no one's responsibility. The increased scrutiny of research facilities
disrupted emotional bonds between research personnel as
well as between personnel and animals. It turned former
colleagues into subordinates or super-ordinates. It could
transform what was once a world of trust and easy dialogue
into one of suspicion and self-protection. Animal care staff,
including even Cramer and his superiors, were afraid to
report problems in the animal holding facilities for fear
they would be penalized. "We used to have a collegial relationship with the USDA," Cramer once told me. "If there
was a problem, I'd tell them and we'd work it out together.
Now it's an adversarial relationship." Cramer spoke of laboratory animal welfare as a game in which one shielded
oneself and sometimes one's colleagues from taking responsibility for criticism. This was reflected in the aggressive language he used when advising his technicians: "Stay
on 'em"; "Push back a little"; "Get out the big clubs."
It was further reflected in the militaristic language that
he used to describe the research staff. He called the principal investigator "Captain," the post-doctoral students
"mouse lieutenants," the part-time summer research assistants "troops," and the university spokespersons "bullet
proof shields," and he referred to the animal care staff as
being "in the trenches."

It was easy to delegate responsibility because animal
research was a fragmented process. Tasks were divided
among investigators, research assistants, technicians, and

animal care staff. Animal research was geographically fragmented also. Some departments had their own holding
facilities and laboratories. The committee found it particularly difficult to enforce regulations once the animals left
the central holding facilities. One committee member
commented: "Each experimenter is responsible for his
own staff and the experimenters have varying degrees of
interest. And an experimenter may have a lab worker who
picks up a rat or a mouse by the tail and dangles him
and the experimenter isn't around to see this." Such serious violations were discovered only accidentally on unan-
nounced walk-throughs. Even then, it was difficult to find
out who was responsible. I recall, for instance, late one
afternoon, when an inspection tour was coming to an end.
Weiss, Cramer, another member of the committee, and I
passed a room in which a young man and woman were
staring animatedly into a glass jar filled with water, watching a white rat swimming in figures of eight, its back legs
pumping furiously. Every so often, the rat disappeared under the water and then resurfaced. "I hope they're not
letting it drown," Weiss commented. We walked further
down the corridor to another room. As Cramer entered, a
young man brushed past him and told him curtly, "There's
an experiment going on in here." Cramer went into the
room and found a rat hooked by electrodes to a computer
that was administering shocks. "Pay attention to the rat
when he's getting shocked," Cramer called out sternly to
the youth, who was now striding down the corridor toward
the room where the other rat was swimming. The youth
returned with a chair and a yellow legal-sized notepad. He
went into the shock room and slammed the door in Cra-

mer's face. Cramer opened the door and, flushed with
rage, said, "Number one: Control your temper! Number
two: Do you know what's going on? This is an inspection of
the Institutional Animal Care and Use Committee. I can
shut you down. I'm sure your supervisor wouldn't want
that." The youth said something, but his voice was too
muffled to hear outside in the corridor where I was standing. Cramer's voice softened, "I know you didn't know that.
Where's your supervisor?" Weiss explained to me that
probably this was a summer assistant and the investigator
was on leave and had not told him that he should not have
left the rat in a room alone while it was getting shocked. "It
wasn't his fault," Weiss emphasized. Cramer believed that
techs and caretakers often took the blame for investigators' failure to explain the regulations. Or, because of the
power and prestige that investigators held over animal
caretakers and techs, they were likely to have "white-coat
syndrome," in which they would listen only to the investigator rather than attend to the regulations.

Relationships with Investigators

Committee members were confused about whether or
not they should be judging the scientific merit of the experiments that investigators submitted to them for review.
They preferred to rely on the funding agencies to do this.
But this was not always possible. Agencies usually required
the committee's approval before they would consider
funding a project. And where animals were used for teaching purposes, there were no agencies on which the committee could rely. These situations presented problems for

the committee in their relationships with investigators because committee members felt that they did not always have the specialized scientific background to judge the merits of the investigators' work. The committee members were put in a position in which they wielded power over investigators without the scientific authority to go with it. While they found most investigators compliant with their suggestions, there were a few who fought against them. Weiss described researchers who seemed to make a game out of challenging the committee. "He likes to be difficult with vengeance," Weiss said of one investigator. "He takes it as almost a challenge. He turns in forms that say nothing. He just says, 'I'm going to use mice to study immunogenetics.' But he's not going to say how many mice and how and why. So you call him up and he goes on for thirty minutes, every time — I've done this three times now — about how stupid the regulations are and how he is an expert."

Surgeons hold particular sway over the committee in this respect. Surgeons at the College Town medical school used animals to teach surgical techniques. Two committee members, however, were reluctant to allow animals to be used in teaching because, they figured, the same procedures were carried out repeatedly, year after year, so they derived no new knowledge. Using animals for teaching was also controversial among the public. Yet it was difficult to challenge surgeons on the necessity of using animals and there was no agency to consult because the university funded teaching. Weiss knew that, when asked for opinions about their colleagues' work, surgeons would support one another because they were reluctant to criticize their peers or superiors. He believed that the chair of the committee was inclined to give the surgeons the benefit of the doubt based on their tenured faculty status and peer-reviewed publications alone.

Unable to systematically evaluate the merits of animal research or violations that occurred outside their purview, the committee members in the College Town ended up paying great attention to things they could monitor, no matter how seemingly trivial, down to the chipped red paint on the pig pens. Even the spelling and grammar on application forms to undertake animal research became serious indicators that a researcher might not be taking the regulations seriously.

Because the regulations did not seem relevant in the light of their relationships with animals, researchers, and care staff, the research ethics committee had to, in a sense, be unethical by violating them. While, on occasion, this appeared to suit the animals as much as it did the research personnel, it made it easier for animal rights activists to accuse the university of failing to take the regulations seriously. In the Perspectives on Animal Research symposium at the College Town, for instance, animal rights activists accused the university of violating regulations by housing its monkeys in single cages. This, they argued, deprived the monkeys of companionship. Pro-research activists rushed to the IACUC's defense by blaming the regulations for the primates' suffering. When animal-care staff housed the monkeys together, they argued, the monkeys would experience greater separation anxiety, since researchers frequently needed to take them in and out of the cages for experiments. "It's not that anyone is opposed to the theory that it's better, under normal conditions, to house animals socially," Glen Alder explained to the animal rights activists. "It's the fact that the regulations are worded so there is no flexibility for the veterination to say, in this case, that isn't necessarily the best for the animals."

It became apparent as I shadowed the IACUC and the university veterinarian that senior administrators were responding to an image of animal welfare and animal research that was at odds with the experience of those who actually enforced the regulations every day. In this image, animals uniformly liked sterile environments, research personnel had a common interest to report regulations, and highly specialized science was readily understood by nonexperts. But as sociologist Donileen R. Loseke aptly concludes in another context, "Policies are not applied to 'images,' they are applied to concrete situations, and there can be important differences between images informing policies and the reality of actual contacts."[2]

Despite the apparent irrelevance of the regulations that were designed to protect animals, such laws unintentionally served other purposes in the College Town. High-ranking university administrators and public relations officers used them to show how humane they were for adhering to them. Researchers and laboratory animal care staff blamed and discredited the animal rights activists for promoting them. And animal rights activists questioned the humanity of the research community for criticizing them.

Conclusion

Feeling Traps

Until now, I have talked about animal rights activists and research supporters in their respective worlds. Yet it is when these parties come together that each side perpetuates the other's shame. Conflicts escalate, according to Thomas Scheff, when there is no mechanism for individuals to express shame and shame is transmuted to anger and pride, which, in turn, can lead to more shame. To block this "feeling trap" — as Scheff calls it — it is necessary to reduce alienation between groups and find ways to offer apology and restitution, whether in a college town or in international politics. Images of Chancellor Willy Brandt spontaneously kneeling and weeping during his visit to the Warsaw Ghetto, for example, are worth far more than the monetary reparations Germany paid to Holocaust survivors.[1] Just as a simple letter of remorse was worth far more to Japan's war victims, the comfort women, than the twenty-thousand-dollar compensation package the government offered them.[2]

The early animal rights activists' demands were very simple too. They wanted researchers to stop using animals from the community shelters. The community, they believed, was betraying its abandoned pets by selling them to research. Here was an opportunity for researchers to publicly acknowledge the moral cost of using animals in medical experiments. They could have shared the animal rights activists' shame by refusing to use pound animals. Researchers considered this option, but only grudgingly.

The shelter's animals were cheaper than animals that had been specially bred for scientific research — $5 each, instead of $175. But it was pride, not money, that discouraged Rachel Rosenthal from breeding her own animals. In fact, the university offered her the money to breed her own. "The principle was of concern to me," Rosenthal explained. Instead of showing conciliation or humility in her early dealings with the animal rights activists, Rosenthal chose pride. She agreed, she said, to "speak for science" at the shelter board's hearing to defend using pound animals in medical experiments. She called her colleagues in the research community to extol the benefits of animal research. Moreover, Rosenthal told the board that they would make "hypocrites of the community" if they banned the use of pound animals in research while reaping its benefits.

Accusing the animal rights activists of being anti-science or hypocritical humiliated them over their emotions toward pets. It encouraged them to find other medical experts to challenge the animal researchers. As the controversy spiraled, Rosenthal surrounded herself with Nobel Prize winners and made much of the fact that she had to build elaborate security systems to protect herself and her laboratory from terrorist attacks. All this played into the hands of animal rights activists, who could then clearly point to the animal researchers as being arrogant, caring only about their prestige, and being secretive and ashamed about animal research.

The closest animal researchers came to publicly showing moral ambivalence over animal experiments was in pro-research symposia. But here, their shame was not believable because it was either transmuted to pride or deferred to the animal rights activists through denunciations of them as terrorists. Or their shame was merely cosmetic — a public relations exercise. "Like it or not," pro-research journalist Katie McCabe told animal researchers when she advised them to show their concern for animals, "this is an emotional issue. It is a public relations battle for the hearts and minds of the public, and, as uncomfortable as this makes you feel as scientists, I believe people's hearts must be won before they will listen to the substance of your arguments. . . . The lay public is quick to accept the emotionally appealing one-liners of the activists, and the negative image of scientists and science."[3] But what McCabe fails to acknowledge is that to diffuse conflicts, apologies should be felt, not merely said.[4] Moreover, McCabe's comments insult both animal rights activists and the broader public by accusing them of being easily led by their emotions rather than their intellect.

Animal rights activists may be more convinced by the kind of emotion that sociologist Arnold Arluke observed in his studies of animal research technicians. All around the lab he found evidence of attachments and appreciation for animals. The researchers memorialized some animals in photographs. They spared others from sacrifice, gave them names, and even kept some of them as pets.[5] Would such gestures appease animal rights activists? Maybe not all. But they did appease Saul, a respected member of the animal rights community, who observed one such lab on a tour of the animal holding facilities in the College Town. "There was a room full of kittens," he recalled. "And all these students thought the kittens were beautiful, because this one room was full of toys hanging from the ceiling. And I thought, 'Dr. Spalding, I've really got to commend you. This is really a thoughtful room.'"

"Oh, it's because one of the lab technicians is a bleeding hearts type," one of the tour guides explained to him.

Instead of capitalizing on these labs, researchers scorned them. They viewed them as amateurish, appropriate only to graduate students.[6] Indeed, although the technicians Arluke studied described feelings that resembled "guilt" over animal experiments, they did not want him to use that word in his report, as if publicly admitting this feeling would further stigmatize them.[7] This illustrates just how alienated animal researchers have become from the public. Animal rights activists, I think, have been more successful than animal researchers in capturing public attention because they have so convincingly articulated the guilt and shame that many people do feel about exploiting animals. And they have helped their followers transmute this shame to more acceptable feelings.

Although I cannot draw any conclusions about the larger and better funded animal rights organizations, for the grass-roots organizations like Animals Anon, it is clear that small, symbolic concessions to the activists can diffuse the controversy. Once certain research proposals were made public in the College Town, few animal rights activists asked to inspect them. Once they were given the feeling that they could participate if they wanted, they lost interest in the issue. Moreover, the activists were easily distracted by other campaigns in which victories of this symbolic kind, rather than the abolition of entire animal research programs, were more likely. Mysteriously, the Larger City university announced that Rosenthal had stopped using cats in her research. The Larger City activists never followed up to find out if this was true. Nor did they reopen the pound seizure issue. Instead, their attention was drawn to another incident. People for the Ethical Treatment of Animals (PETA) sent an undercover agent to an animal dealer who sold animals to schools for dissection. A man was seen stealing away from the facilities with a gas chamber. A pile of collars suggested the animals being sold had been pets. The thought of school children dissecting pets, secretly killed in a gas chamber — like the Jews in Germany — distracted Animals Anon from Rosenthal's research and pound seizure. This campaign attracted more support than the one against Rosenthal, including from the humane societies, precisely because it did not appear anti-science.

Animal rights activists were also responsible for perpetuating the opposition's isolation and shame. As with the animal researchers, there were moments when animal rights activists could have achieved their objectives without escalating the conflict. When activists failed to stop the shelter from selling its animals to research, they began to protest Rosenthal. At the time, Dee wanted only to stop Rosenthal's experiments. She did not oppose all animal research. Dee recalls her own shame when coming to David Nathan's office to ask that Rosenthal's work be stopped. "I think back then we were looked upon as a joke. We were seen as a

bunch of bored people with nothing else to do," she told
me.

At first, Nathan helped Dee overcome her uneasiness.
"Well, actually, he was very nice and very cordial," she admitted. "One thing he was not—he was not condescend-
ing. Which I sort of expected him to be. I thought he was
really an OK guy. He was doing his job. But since then, he's
not been too OK." So what happened to disrupt these
congenial relations? Because the animal rights activists
were not willing to accept his compromise of using labora-
tory-bred animals for research instead of pound animals,
Nathan concluded that they were against all animal research. "It made me mad," he told me, his voice bristling
with rage. "It made me EXTREMELY mad. Because I'm willing to talk to people. If they want to protest us doing something, I'm willing to discuss how we do it. And if they've got
a constructive suggestion for another way to do it, we'll
listen. But they're totally abolitionist, without admitting
it." To Nathan, the animal rights activists were being dis-
honest because they denied their initial feelings about
using abandoned pets in research. Nathan felt angry and
isolated—after he had tried to help the activists save face.
"How can you deal with people like this?" he asked me.
"Unfortunately, I was in the meeting by myself. Five of
them and one of me. So I dropped the matter." At that
point, Dee launched the vociferous publicity and letter-
writing campaign against the university—which made university officials more reluctant to talk openly about animal
research.

Animal rights activists, like the researchers, could have
avoided conflict by acknowledging their own role in animal

suffering, rather than pinning blame on others. They might have talked more about their own failings — the kinds of things that they told me about not always being able to live completely cruelty-free lives. Such admissions might have encouraged animal researchers to express their shame too and therefore make them less likely to close their doors, to harp self-righteously on the benefits of animal research, and to deride animal rights activists. Even animal rights activists who were totally abolitionist could have acknowledged that it is difficult to lead a life that is unaffected by animal use. At the height of the campaign against Rosenthal, research supporters came face to face with animal rights activists across the protest lines. After formal speeches, the two groups began to mingle. Several pro-research graduate students congregated around Kate, an animal rights supporter who was giving out literature and wearing a badge with Rosenthal's name struck out with a red line like a prohibitive road sign. Notice how Kate, while wriggling out of admitting that she herself benefited from animal research, shamed animal researchers and thus fueled their pride.

Kate: Theoretically, I would like to see all animal research stop — when I look at my own pets, my own bird. And one of the questions people ask me is, "If your kid was dying, would you protest animal research?" Another question, that I asked the researchers at the Joseph Bennet Medical Center is, "Would you do the research that you do on the pets you get from the Johnsonville Shelter on your own pet?" And they all went real red, and no one said anything. But I think it's the same kind of question.

1st grad student: At the same time I thank God that they did the research because my dog is alive today and almost got parvovirus.

Kate: But how many dogs died so your dog could be saved?

1st grad student: But still, that's my dog. Just like I wouldn't want humans not to have that vaccine. And it's not just my dog. It's everybody's dog who's alive today.

2d grad student: Certainly people who advocate animal rights will take that vaccine — they do, don't they?

Kate: Slavery. Everyone thought that that was fun. People still think that's fun. The Ku Klux Klan still marches because they think they have the right to . . .

3d grad student (interrupting): You really believe that you can compare your cause with people that were killed in the Holocaust? You really believe that you can compare, in the newspaper, your cause with the blacks in slavery!

Kate: We do.

4th grad student (pointing to Kate's leather shoes): But you're wearing a dead animal right now.

Kate: So are a lot of people.

3d grad student: You're wearing makeup that has been tested on animals.

4th grad student: You're wearing leather now.

Kate (looking apologetic): I know.

A bystander: Do you eat meat?

Kate (still looking apologetic): No.

Another bystander: Do you eat fish?

Kate: No. My mother bought these things [*pointing to her shoes*] for my birthday one year.

4th grad student: Well, don't wear them then!

Kate: You know what's funny? You know why I have these on today? I don't usually wear them. But I'm pregnant and my feet are so swollen. They're the only thing that I have.

1st grad student: Well, AIDS patients are going to say that the only thing that's going to make me live is if I can find a cure through animal research. I mean 50 percent of us would all be dead without animal research.

Kate never acknowledged her shame. She began with a triumphant story about how she shamed researchers for experimenting on pets. When the graduate students tried to push her into acknowledging that by wearing leather, she, like the researchers was responsible for animal suffering, she fended them off. First, she changed the subject altogether to slavery, suggesting that researchers are like the Ku Klux Klan. Then she said that she did not buy her leather shoes, her mother did. She blamed her mother. Finally, she passed her shame to her unborn baby. This parceling out of shame only encouraged pride in the pro-research activists. Rather than admitting their ambivalence toward animal research, the four graduate students extolled its benefits to all.

Animal rights activists could have acknowledged researchers' shame also. In recalling her meeting with Nathan, Dee laughed at Nathan's outburst. The Larger City chapter frequently laughed at Rosenthal's "paranoia." Animal rights activists held scientists to the nonemotional ideal that they wanted to emulate. They then derided scientists for failing to live up to this ideal. "It always amazes me," Douglas declared amidst whistles, jeers, and shrieks of delight from animal rights activists outside Rosenthal's

lab, "that our opponents accuse us of being overly sentimental, of being misinformed." He gestured toward researchers standing sheepishly with pictures of children
saved by animal research. "Yet the three pictures that they
are always working with, and that you see here today are, in
my humble opinion, classic examples of mushy sentimentality and distorted propaganda!" Such comments belittle
researchers' emotions, wherein it is emotional sensitivity
that is at stake in the controversy.

The media heightens both parties' isolation and shame.
Shortly after the Farm raid, College Town university officials became fearful of talking with the public about the
animal rights activists' accusations and opening their labs
to public inspection in case animal rights activists made
sensationalist claims to the media about animal cruelty.
Saul recalls how he and another animal rights activist from
the College Town student group sat on a stone wall outside
the medical school library talking to a medical student that
they met during a restricted tour of the animal-holding
facilities. During the tour, a rabbit had struggled against a
technician who tried to pick it up. The students sat talking
as the sun began to turn red and wafts of warm air escaped
from the concrete surfaces of the med school complex and
funneled through the campus buildings. The fear and isolation that the press had created between them became
apparent. "I was left with one medical student, which was
actually his first introduction to animal rights, and he was
quite interested," Saul said.

> We sat for an hour talking about what our fears
> were of each other and what their concerns were.

And at that point he said, "Well, we just don't know what you're doing. We don't know who we're talking to. You say that this could all go to the press. We know that next week's Animal Liberation Day and you know that a rabbit freaked out in the lab tech's hands while we were on the tour. We don't know what happened, but it sounded like it was put into a meat grinder. How do we know you're not going to make any press releases?"

"You're just going to have to trust us," Saul told him. Saul did not call the press. Some College Town activists scolded him for it. But he did manage to negotiate a contract with a local grocery store to get better food for the primates, and he persuaded animal caretakers to install a television for them. Animal rights activists and research supporters reached agreements in these informal encounters. But both sides appeared most extremist when challenged in public settings. If animal rights activists go on public record as saying that they support only some types of animal use, they will be shamed by pro-researchers and other animal rights activists for being hypocritical. And if research supporters go on record as supporting some animal rights claims, they fear they will be crediting the animal rights movement and thus betraying their profession. The most successful negotiations, as Thomas Scheff points out, go on in private, between small groups, rather than large ones. Negotiations between Palestinians and Israelis, for instance, moved quickly in the early stages, when key individuals met in secret locations in Norway. But when the negotiations took place in public, in large conferences in front of television cameras, Arabs and Israelis made speeches designed to publicly denounce one another.[8]

As we search for ever more efficient and healthy lifestyles, we have become increasingly dependent on animals, while developing more humane and caring feelings toward them. Most of us never fully resolve the contradiction between using animals as commodities and keeping them as pets. We can probably all recall feeling uneasy about eating food that resembles the animal it came from, or turning our faces away from abhorrent pictures of slaughterhouses or animal experiments. Out of such moral ambivalence grows shame, guilt, and alienation, often expressed in pride, self-righteousness, and anger. Grass-roots social movements can provoke these feelings more effectively than before, with the help of multimedia communication.

We might not have much control over the causes of our uneasinesss about animal use. But a resolution of the animal research controversy can still be reached if we manage our shame in ways that do not lead to the feeling traps that I describe.

$\mathscr{N}otes$

INTRODUCTION: SHAME

1. P. J. O'Rourke, *All the Troubles in the World: The Lighter Side of Famine, Pestilence, Destruction, and Death* (London: Picador, 1995), 4.

2. Alison M. Jaggar, "Love and Knowledge: Emotion in the Feminist Epistemology," in *Gender/Body/Knowledge: Feminist Reconstructions of Being and Knowing*, edited by Alison M. Jagger and Susan R. Bordo (New Brunswick, N.J.: Rutgers University Press, 1992).

3. Sherryl Kleinman and Martha A. Copp, *Emotions and Fieldwork* (Newbury Park, Calif.: Sage, 1993).

4. See, for example, Aldon D. Morris and Carol McClurg Mueller, eds., *Frontiers in Social Movement Theory* (New Haven, Conn.: Yale University Press, 1992); Enrique Laraña, Hank Johnston, and Joseph R. Gusfield, eds., *New Social Movements: From Ideology to Identity* (Philadelphia: Temple University Press, 1994); Scott A. Hunt and Robert D. Benford, "Identity Talk in the Peace and Justice Movement," *Journal of Contemporary Ethnography* 22 (1994): 488–517.

5. For an exception, see Craig Calhoun, *Neither Gods nor Emperors: Students and the Struggle for Democracy in China* (Berkeley: University of California Press, 1994).

6. See Thomas J. Scheff and Suzanne M. Retzinger, *Emotions and Violence: Shame and Rage in Destructive Conflicts* (Lexington, Mass.: Lexington Books, 1991),

and Thomas J. Scheff, *Bloody Revenge: Emotions, Nationalism, and War* (Boulder, Colo.: Westview Press, 1994).

7. Scheff, *Bloody Revenge*, 40.

8. Ibid., 53.

9. Ibid., 107.

10. Ibid., 116.

11. Ibid., 118.

12. Ibid., 120.

13. Mario Jacoby, *Shame and the Origins of Self-Esteem: A Jungian Approach* (London: Routledge, 1994); Susan Miller, *The Shame Experience* (Hillsdale, N.J.: The Analytic Press, 1993).

14. Michael Lewis, *Shame: The Exposed Self* (New York: The Free Press, 1992).

15. Léon Wurmser, *The Mask of Shame* (Baltimore, Md.: Johns Hopkins University Press, 1981).

16. Scheff and Retzinger, *Emotions and Violence*.

17. Quoted in O'Rourke, *All the Troubles*, 171.

18. David A. E. Snow, Burke Rochford Jr., Steven K. Worden, and Robert D. Benford, "Frame Alignment Processes, Micromobilization, and Movement Participation," *American Sociological Review* 51 (1986): 464–81.

19. "A Crisis of Conscience," *The Economist*, July 22, 1995.

20. Ralph Turner, "The Real Self: From Institution to Impulse," *American Journal of Sociology* 81 (1976): 989–1016; Arlie Russell Hochschild, *The Managed Heart: The Commercialization of Human Feeling* (Berkeley: University of California Press, 1983).

21. Robert Jackall, *Moral Mazes: The World of Corporate Managers* (New York: Oxford University Press, 1988).

22. See, for example, Carol Gilligan, *In a Different Voice: Psychological Theory and Women's Development* (Cambridge, Mass.: Harvard University Press, 1982).

23. See Ian Buruma, *The Wages of Guilt: Memories of War in Germany and Japan* (New York: Farrar, Straus & Giroux, 1994).

24. Robert Bly, *Iron John* (Reading, Mass.: Addison-Wesley, 1990), 6.

25. Sherryl Kleinman, *Equals Before God: Seminarians as Humanistic Professionals* (Chicago: University of Chicago Press, 1984).

26. Mary Field Belenky, Blythe McVicker Clinchy, Nancy Rule Goldberger, and Jill Mattuck Tarule, *Women's Ways of Knowing: The Development of Self, Voice, and Mind* (New York: Basic Books, 1986), 91, 93.

27. See, for example, Camille Paglia, *Sex, Art, and American Culture: Essays* (New York: Vintage Books, 1992).

28. For a review of these writers, see Steven Seidman, *Contested Knowledge: Social Theory in the Postmodern Era* (Cambridge, Mass.: Blackwell, 1994), chap. 7.

29. See, for example, Susan Sperling, *Animal Liberators: Research and Morality* (Berkeley: University of California Press, 1988); James M. Jasper and Jane Poulsen, "Animal Rights and Anti-Nuclear Protest: Condensing Symbols and the Critique of Instrumental Reason" (paper presented at the annual meeting of the American Sociological Association, San Francisco, August 1989); and James M. Jasper and Dorothy Nelkin, *The Animal Rights Crusade: The Growth of a Moral Protest* (New York: The Free Press, 1992).

30. Katie McCabe, "The Growing Power of the Animal Rights Movement" (paper presented at a meeting of the Board of Governors of the California Biomedical Research Association, July 1987).

31. "What Humans Owe to Animals," *The Economist*, August 19, 1995.

ONE: THE ACTIVISTS AND I

1. See, for example, Susan Sperling, *Animal Liberators: Research and Morality* (Berkeley: University of California Press, 1988); James M. Jasper and Jane Poulsen, "Animal Rights and Anti-Nuclear Protest: Condensing Symbols and the Critique of Instrumental Reason" (paper presented at the annual meeting of the American Sociological Association, San Francisco, August 1989); and James M. Jasper and Dorothy Nelkin, *The Animal Rights Crusade: The Growth of a Moral Protest* (New York: The Free Press, 1992).

2. See, for example, Charles S. Nicoll and Sharon Russell, "Editorial: Analysis of Animal Rights Literature Reveals the Underlying Motives of the Move-

ment: Ammunition for Counter Offensive by Scientists," *Endocrinology* 127 (1990): 985–89.

3. See, for example, Thomas F. Gieryn, "Boundary-Work and the Demarcation of Science from Non-Science: Strains and Interests in Professional Ideologies of Scientists," *American Sociological Review* 48 (1983): 781 – 95, and Mike Michael and Lynda Birke, "Enrolling the Core Set: The Case of the Animal Experimentation Controversy," *Social Studies of Science* 24 (1994): 81 – 95.

4. See, for example, David A. Snow, "A Dramaturgical Analysis of Movement Accommodation: Building Idiosyncrasy Credit as a Movement Strategy," *Symbolic Interaction* 2 (1979): 23–44; Joseph R. Gusfield, *The Culture of Public Problems: Drinking-Driving and the Symbolic Order* (Chicago: University of Chicago Press, 1981); and Joel Best, ed., *Images of Issues: Typifying Contemporary Social Problems* (New York: Aldine de Gruyter, 1989).

5. James P. Spradley, *Participant Observation* (Fort Worth, Tex.: Holt, Rinehart and Winston, 1980).

6. Katie McCabe, "Beyond Cruelty," *The Washingtonian*, February 1990, 73–195.

7. John Lofland, *Doomsday Cult: A Study of Conversion: Proselytization, and Maintenance of Faith*, enlarged edition (New York: Irvington-Wiley, 1977).

8. Sherryl Kleinman and Martha A. Copp, *Emotions and Fieldwork* (Newbury Park, Calif.: Sage, 1993), 6.

9. See, for example, Susan Kreiger, "Beyond 'Subjectivity': The Use of the Self in Social Science," *Qualitative Sociology* 8 (1985): 309–24, and Kleinman and Copp, *Emotions and Fieldwork*.

10. Lawrence Finsen and Susan Finsen, *The Animal Rights Movement in America: From Compassion to Respect* (New York: Twayne Publishers, 1994), xiv.

11. Sperling, *Animal Liberators*, 7–8.

12. Ibid., 15.

13. For a summary of these, see John Broida, Leanne Tingley, Robert Kimball, and Joseph Miele, "Personality Differences Between Pro- and Anti-Vivisectionists," *Society and Animals* 1, no. 2 (1993): 129–44.

14. See, for example, Jasper and Nelkin, *Animal Rights Crusade.*

15. See, for example, Michael and Birke, "Enrolling the Core Set."

16. See also Corwin R. Kruse, "Images, Ideas, and Context: Media Framing and the Construction of the Animal Experimentation Debate" (master's thesis, Pennsylvania State University, 1995, 8–10, who points this out with respect to media coverage of the animal rights controversy, citing Michael Billig, *Arguing and Thinking: A Rhetorical Approach to Social Psychology* (Cambridge: Cambridge University Press, 1987), and Michael Billig, *Ideology and Opinions: Studies in Rhetorical Psychology* (London: Sage, 1991).

17. I use the broad term *animal protection* to denote both the animal welfare and the animal rights positions. Briefly stated, animal welfare supporters promote kindness to animals, although they are not necessarily against all forms of animal use. Some animal welfarists, for example, eat meat, wear animal products, and support some kinds of animal research. Followers of the animal welfare tradition include local humane societies, the Society for the Prevention of Cruelty to Animals (SPCA), and animal welfare leagues. Strict followers of the animal rights philosophy believe that animals have intrinsic rights that should be guaranteed just as they are for people. These rights include not being killed, eaten, or used for sport or animal experimentation. Followers of this tradition include People for the Ethical Treatment of Animals (PETA), the Animal Liberation Front (ALF), and local and national antivivisection societies.

TWO: THE HUMAN DILEMMA

1. James A. Serpell, "Pet Keeping in Non-Western Societies: Some Popular Misconceptions," in *Animals and People Sharing the World*, edited by Andrew N. Rowan (Hanover, N.H.: University Press of New England, 1988), 41–42.

2. Keith Thomas, *Man and the Natural World* (New York: Pantheon, 1983).

3. Quoted in ibid., 29.

4. Quoted in ibid., 35.

5. James Turner, *Reckoning with the Beast: Animals, Pain, and Humanity in the Victorian Mind* (Baltimore, Md.: Johns Hopkins University Press, 1980), 785.

6. See, for example, ibid.; Richard D. French, *Anti-Vivisection and Medical Science in Victorian Society* (Princeton, N.J.: Princeton University Press, 1975); Mary Ann Elston, "Woman and Anti-Vivisection in Victorian England, 1870–1900," in *Vivisection in Historical Perspective*, edited by Nicholas A. Rupke (London: Croom Helm, 1987), 259–83; and Susan Sperling, *Animal Liberators: Research and Morality* (Berkeley: University of California Press, 1988).

7. Mary P. Ryan, "Gender and Public Access: Women's Politics in Nineteenth-Century America," in *Habermas and the Public Sphere*, edited by Craig Calhoun (Cambridge, Mass.: MIT Press, 1992), 259–88.

8. Quoted in James M. Jasper and Dorothy Nelkin, *The Animal Rights Crusade: The Growth of a Moral Protest* (New York: The Free Press, 1992), 59.

9. Turner, *Reckoning with the Beast*, 55.

10. Sperling, *Animal Liberators*.

11. Turner, *Reckoning with the Beast*, 97.

12. Quoted in Josephine Donovan, "Animal Rights and Feminist Theory," in *Ecofeminism: Women, Animals, Nature*, edited by Greta Gaard (Philadelphia: Temple University Press, 1993), 168.

13. Jasper and Nelkin, *Animal Rights Crusade*.

14. Talcott Parsons quoted in Mary P. Ryan, *Womanhood in America*, 3d ed. (New York: Watts, 1983), 261.

15. Jasper and Nelkin, *Animal Rights Crusade*.

16. Ibid.

17. Ibid.

18. Peter Singer, *Animal Liberation: A New Ethics for Our Treatment of Animals* (New York: Avon Books, 1975), xi.

19. Lawrence Finsen and Susan Finsen, *The Animal Rights Movement in America: From Compassion to Respect* (New York: Twayne Publishers, 1994).

20. Ibid.

21. Jasper and Nelkin, *Animal Rights Crusade*.

22. "People for the Ethical Treatment of Animals," *Animal Times* 11, no. 1 (spring 1996): 23.

23. For a fuller description of the different types of organizations, see Finsen and Finsen, *The Animal Rights Movement in America.*

24. Susan Sperling, *Animal Liberators.*

25. For a review of these stereotypes, see John Broida, Leanne Tingley, Robert Kimball, and Joseph Miele, "Personality Differences Between Pro- and Anti-Vivisectionists," *Society and Animals* 1, no. 2 (1993): 129–44.

26. James M. Jasper and Jane Poulsen, "Animal Rights and Anti-Nuclear Protest: Condensing Symbols and the Critique of Instrumental Reason" (paper presented at the annual meeting of the American Sociological Association, San Francisco, August 1989); Jasper and Nelkin, *Animal Rights Crusade.*

27. Carol Gilligan, *In a Different Voice: Psychological Theory and Women's Development* (Cambridge, Mass.: Harvard University Press, 1982).

28. Reuther, Lauter, Merchant, and Ruddick are all quoted in Donovan, "Animal Rights and Feminist Theory," 180, 182, 174, 183, respectively.

29. Carol J. Adams, "The Feminist Traffic in Animals," in Gaard, *Ecofeminism,* 195–218.

30. Robert Jackall, *Moral Mazes: The World of Corporate Managers* (New York: Oxford University Press, 1988).

31. Quoted in Andreas-Holger Maehle and Ulrich Thröhler, "Animal Experimentation from Antiquity to the End of the Eighteenth Century: Attitudes and Arguments," in Rupke, *Vivisection in Historical Perspective,* 15.

32. Quoted in ibid., 19.

33. Quoted in ibid., 18.

34. Quoted in ibid., 27.

35. Quoted in French, *Anti-Vivisection,* 20.

36. Stewart Richards, "Vicarious Suffering, Necessary Pain: Physiological Method in Late Nineteenth-Century Britain," in Rupke, *Vivisection in Historical Perspective,* 125–48.

37. Nicholaas A. Rupke, "Pro-Vivisection in England in the Early 1880s: Arguments and Motives," in Rupke, *Vivisection in Historical Perspective,* 200.

38. See Turner, *Reckoning with the Beast,* and Susan E. Lederer, "The Contro-

versy over Animal Experimentation in America, 1880–1914," in Rupke, *Vivisection in Historical Perspective*, 236–58.

39. Susan E. Lederer, "Political Animals: The Shaping of Biomedical Research Literature in Twentieth-Century America," *ISIS* 83, no. 1 (1992): 70.

40. Robert Zussman, *Intensive Care: Medical Ethics and the Medical Profession* (Chicago: University of Chicago Press, 1992).

41. Mary T. Phillips and Jeri A. Sechzer, *Animal Research and Ethical Conflict: An Analysis of the Scientific Literature, 1966–1986* (New York: Springer-Verlag, 1989).

42. Ibid.

43. Arnold Arluke, "Uneasiness Among Laboratory Technicians," *Lab Animal* 19 (May–June 1990): 21–39; Arnold Arluke, "Going into the Closet with Science: Information Control Among Animal Experimenters," *Journal of Contemporary Ethnography* 20 (1991): 306–30.

44. Donovan, "Animal Rights and Feminist Theory."

45. For examples of such perspectives, see journals such as *Society and Animals* and *Anthrozoös*.

46. Thomas, *Man and the Natural World*, 301.

THREE: THE COLLEGE TOWN

1. Faye D. Ginsburg, *Contested Lives: The Abortion Debate in an American Community* (Berkeley: University of California Press, 1989).

2. I will use first names to denote animal rights activists and surnames to denote animal research supporters in order to clarify which side of the controversy a person is on. Researchers are seldom known by their first names.

3. James M. Jasper and Dorothy Nelkin, *The Animal Rights Crusade: The Growth of a Moral Protest* (New York: The Free Press, 1992), 172–73.

4. See ibid., and Susan Sperling, *Animal Liberators: Research and Morality* (Berkeley: University of California Press, 1988).

5. Harold A. Herzog, Jr., " 'The Movement Is My Life': The Psychology of Animal Rights Activism," *Journal of Social Issues* 49, no. 1 (1993): 103–19.

FOUR: ALL OUR SINS

1. Peter L. Berger, *The Capitalist Revolution* (Aldershot, Eng.: Wildwood House, 1987).

2. Tom Regan, *The Struggle for Animal Rights* (Clarks Summit, Pa.: International Society for Animal Rights, Inc., 1987), 117.

3. Joseph R. Gusfield, *The Culture of Public Problems: Drinking-Driving and the Symbolic Order* (Chicago: University of Chicago Press, 1981).

4. Arlie Russell Hochschild, *The Managed Heart: The Commercialization of Human Feeling* (Berkeley: University of California Press, 1983), 83.

5. The disruption that the animal rights movement created in activists' personal lives has also been observed by Harold A. Herzog Jr., " 'The Movement Is My Life': The Psychology of Animal Rights Activism," *Journal of Social Issues* 49, no. 1 (1993): 103–19.

FIVE: STEWARDSHIP AND SCIENCE

1. Mike Michael and Lynda Birke, in "Accounting for Animal Experiments: Identity and Disreputable 'Others,' " *Science, Technology, and Human Values* 19 (spring 1994): 189–204, describe how animal researchers in Britain draw moral boundaries between themselves and other users of animals. But they do not examine the more personal strategies that animal researchers use to distinguish themselves as humane.

2. "Animals and Sickness," *Wall Street Journal*, April 24, 1989, A14.

SIX: LEARNED EMOTION

1. Deborah Tannen, *You Just Don't Understand: Women and Men in Conversation* (New York: Ballantine Books, 1991).

2. Ibid.

3. See Mary Field Belenky, Blythe McVicker Clinchy, Nancy Rule Goldberger, and Jill Mattuck Tarule, *Women's Ways of Knowing: The Development of Self, Voice, and Mind* (New York: Basic Books, 1986), 105.

SEVEN: TELEVISION DOCTORS

1. Arnold Arluke, "Going into the Closet with Science: Information Control Among Animal Experimenters," *Journal of Contemporary Ethnography* 20 (1991): 306–30.

2. Robert J. Denver et al., "Direct Action for Animal Research," *Science* 241 (1988): 11.

3. Arnold Arluke and Julian McAllister Groves, "From Scientists to Ethicists: The Social Construction of Scientists as Moral Agents in the Animal Research Controversy," in *Responsible Conduct of Research in Animal Behavior,* edited by Lynette Hart (New York: Oxford University Press, forthcoming).

4. Katie McCabe, "The Growing Power of the Animal Rights Movement" (paper presented at a meeting of the Board of Governors of the California Biomedical Research Association, July 1987).

5. American Medical Association, "A Miracle at Risk," slide #36 (Chicago, 1992).

6. John A. Kransey, "Some Thoughts on the Value of Life," *Buffalo Physician* 18 (September 1984): 6.

7. See, for example, Ron Karpati, "A Scientist: I Am the Enemy," *Newsweek,* December 18, 1989, 12–13.

8. See Robert J. White, "The Facts About Animal Research," *Reader's Digest,* March 1988, 127–32.

9. John G. Hubbell, *The "Animal Rights" War on Medicine* (Pleasantville, N.Y.: Reader's Digest Association, 1990).

10. Peggy Peck, "The New Abolitionists: Animal Rights Terrorists Strike Medicine," *Physician's Management,* June 1989, 49.

11. Quoted in Katie McCabe, "Who Will Live, Who Will Die?" *The Washingtonian,* August 1986, 114.

12. See, for example, S. Paris, "Letter from the President," *Progress* 1 (1992–1993): 1.

13. Thomas F. Gieryn, "Boundary-Work and the Demarcation of Science

from Non-Science: Strains and Interests in Professional Ideologies of Scientists," *American Sociological Review* 48 (1983): 781–95.

EIGHT: REGULATIONS

1. Karl Mannheim, *Ideology and Utopia: An Introduction to the Sociology of Knowledge* (San Diego: Harcourt Brace Jovanovich, 1985).

2. Donileen R. Loseke, " 'Violence' Is 'Violence' or Is It? The Social Construction of Wife Abuse and Public Policy," in *Images of Issues: Typifying Contemporary Social Problems*, edited by Joel Best (New York: Aldine de Gruyter, 1989), 191–206.

CONCLUSION: FEELING TRAPS

1. Thomas J. Scheff, *Bloody Revenge: Emotions, Nationalism, and War* (Boulder, Colo.: Westview Press, 1994), 143.

2. "Compensation Fails to Ease Comfort Women's Grief," *Hong Kong Standard*, June 6, 1996, 10.

3. Katie McCabe, "The Growing Power of the Animal Rights Movement" (paper presented at a meeting of the Board of Governors of the California Biomedical Research Association, July 1987).

4. Scheff, *Bloody Revenge*, 131.

5. Arnold Arluke, "Moral Elevation in Medical Research," *Advances in Medical Sociology* 1 (1990): 199–204.

6. Mary T. Phillips, "Proper Names and the Construction of Biography: The Case of Laboratory Animals" (paper presented at the annual meeting of the American Sociological Association, Cincinnati, Ohio, August 1991).

7. Arnold Arluke, "Going into the Closet with Science: Information Control Among Animal Experimenters," *Journal of Contemporary Ethnography* 20 (1991): 306–30.

8. Scheff, *Bloody Revenge*, 145.

Bibliography

Adams, Carol J. "The Feminist Traffic in Animals." In *Ecofeminism: Women, Animals, Nature,* edited by Greta Gaard, 195–218. Philadelphia: Temple University Press, 1993.

American Medical Association. "A Miracle at Risk." Slide #36. Chicago, 1992.

"Animals and Sickness." *Wall Street Journal,* April 24, 1989, A14.

Arluke, Arnold. "Going into the Closet with Science: Information Control Among Animal Experimenters." *Journal of Contemporary Ethnography* 20 (1991): 306–30.

———. "Moral Elevation in Medical Research." *Advances in Medical Sociology* 1 (1990): 199–204.

———. "Uneasiness Among Laboratory Technicians." *Lab Animal* 19 (May–June 1990): 21–39.

Arluke, Arnold, and Julian McAllister Groves. "From Scientists to Ethicists: The Social Construction of Scientists as Moral Agents in the Animal Research Controversy." In *Responsible Conduct of Research in Animal Behavior,* edited by Lynette Hart. New York: Oxford University Press, forthcoming.

Belenky, Mary Field, Blythe McVicker Clinchy, Nancy Rule Goldberger, and Jill Mattuck Tarule. *Women's Ways of Knowing: The Development of Self, Voice, and Mind.* New York: Basic Books, 1986.

Berger, Peter L. 1987. *The Capitalist Revolution.* Aldershot, Eng.: Wildwood House, 1987.

Best, Joel, ed. *Images of Issues: Typifying Contemporary Social Problems.* New York: Aldine de Gruyter, 1989.

Billig, Michael. *Arguing and Thinking: A Rhetorical Approach to a Social Psychology.* Cambridge: Cambridge University Press, 1987.

———. *Ideology and Opinions: Studies in Rhetorical Psychology.* London: Sage, 1991.

Bly, Robert. *Iron John.* Reading, Mass.: Addison-Wesley, 1990.

Broida, John, Leanne Tingley, Robert Kimball, and Joseph Miele. "Personality Differences Between Pro- and Anti-Vivisectionists." *Society and Animals* 1, no. 2 (1993): 129–44.

Buruma, Ian. *The Wages of Guilt: Memories of War in Germany and Japan.* New York: Farrar, Straus & Giroux, 1994.

Calhoun, Craig. *Neither Gods nor Emperors: Students and the Struggle for Democracy in China.* Berkeley: University of California Press, 1994.

"Compensation Fails to Ease Comfort Women's Grief." *Hong Kong Standard,* June 6, 1996, 10.

"A Crisis of Conscience." *The Economist,* July 22, 1995.

Denver, Robert J., et al. "Direct Action for Animal Research." *Science* 241 (1988): 11.

Donovan, Josephine. "Animal Rights and Feminist Theory." In *Ecofemi-*

nism: Women, Animals, Nature, edited by Greta Gaard, 167–94. Philadelphia: Temple University Press, 1993.

Elston, Mary Ann. "Women and Anti-Vivisection in Victorian England, 1870–1900." In *Vivisection in Historical Perspective,* edited by Nicholaas A. Rupke, 259–93. London: Croom Helm, 1987.

Finsen, Lawrence, and Susan Finsen. *The Animal Rights Movement in America: From Compassion to Respect.* New York: Twayne Publishers, 1994.

French, Richard D. *Anti-Vivisection and Medical Science in Victorian Society.* Princeton, N.J.: Princeton University Press, 1975.

Gieryn, Thomas F. "Boundary-Work and the Demarcation of Science from Non-Science: Strains and Interests in Professional Ideologies of Scientists." *American Sociological Review* 48 (1983): 781–95.

Gilligan, Carol. *In a Different Voice: Psychological Theory and Women's Development.* Cambridge, Mass.: Harvard University Press, 1982.

Ginsburg, Faye D. *Contested Lives: The Abortion Debate in an American Community.* Berkeley: University of California Press, 1989.

Gusfield, Joseph R. *The Culture of Public Problems: Drinking-Driving and the Symbolic Order.* Chicago: University of Chicago Press, 1981.

Herzog, Harold A. Jr. " 'The Movement Is My Life': The Psychology of Animal Rights Activism." *Journal of Social Issues* 49, no. 1 (1993): 103–19.

Hochschild, Arlie Russell. *The Managed Heart: The Commercialization of Human Feeling.* Berkeley: University of California Press, 1983.

Hubbell, John G. *The "Animal Rights" War on Medicine.* Pleasantville, N.Y.: Reader's Digest Association, 1990.

Hunt, Scott A., and Robert D. Benford. "Identity Talk in the Peace and Justice Movement." *Journal of Contemporary Ethnography* 22 (1994): 488–517.

Jackall, Robert. *Moral Mazes: The World of Corporate Managers.* New York: Oxford University Press, 1988.

Jacoby, Mario. *Shame and the Origins of Self-Esteem: A Jungian Approach.* London: Routledge, 1994.

Jaggar, Alison M. "Love and Knowledge: Emotion in the Feminist Epistemology." In *Gender/Body/Knowledge: Feminist Reconstructions of Being and Knowing,* edited by Alison M. Jaggar and Susan R. Bordo. New Brunswick, N.J.: Rutgers University Press, 1992.

Jasper, James M., and Dorothy Nelkin. *The Animal Rights Crusade: The Growth of a Moral Protest.* New York: The Free Press, 1992.

Jasper, James M., and Jane Poulsen. "Animal Rights and Anti-Nuclear Protest: Condensing Symbols and the Critique of Instrumental Reason." Paper presented at the annual meeting of the American Sociological Association, San Francisco, August 1989.

Karpati, Ron. "A Scientist: I Am the Enemy." *Newsweek,* December 18, 1989, 12–13.

Kleinman, Sherryl. *Equals Before God: Seminarians as Humanistic Professionals.* Chicago: University of Chicago Press, 1984.

Kleinman, Sherryl, and Martha A. Copp. *Emotions and Fieldwork.* Newbury Park, Calif.: Sage, 1993.

Kransey, John A. "Some Thoughts on the Value of Life." *Buffalo Physician* 18 (September 1984): 6–18.

Kreiger, Susan. "Beyond 'Subjectivity': The Use of the Self in Social Science." *Qualitative Sociology* 8 (1985): 309–24.

Kruse, Corwin R. "Images, Ideas, and Context: Media Framing and the Construction of the Animal Experimentation Debate." Master's thesis, Pennsylvania State University, 1995.

Laraña, Enrique, Hank Johnston, and Joseph R. Gusfield, eds. *New Social Movements: From Ideology to Identity.* Philadelphia: Temple University Press, 1994.

Lederer, Susan E. "The Controversy over Animal Experimentation in America, 1880–1914." In *Vivisection in Historical Perspective*, edited by Nicholaas A. Rupke, 236–58. London: Croom Helm, 1987.

———. "Political Animals: The Shaping of Biomedical Research Literature in Twentieth-Century America." *ISIS* 83, no. 1 (1992): 61–80.

Lewis, Michael. *Shame: The Exposed Self.* New York: The Free Press, 1992.

Lofland, John. *Doomsday Cult: A Study of Conversion, Proselytization, and Maintenance of Faith.* Enlarged edition. New York: Irvington-Wiley, 1977.

Loseke, Donileen R. " 'Violence Is 'Violence' or Is It? The Social Construction of Wife Abuse and Public Policy." In *Images of Issues: Typifying Contemporary Social Problems*, edited by Joel Best, 191–206. New York: Aldine de Gruyter, 1989.

Maehle, Andreas-Holger, and Ulrich Tröhler. "Animal Experimentation from Antiquity to the End of the Eighteenth Century: Attitudes and Arguments." In *Vivisection in Historical Perspective*, edited by Nicholaas A. Rupke, 14–47. London: Croom Helm, 1987.

Mannheim, Karl. *Ideology and Utopia: An Introduction to the Sociology of Knowledge.* San Diego: Harcourt Brace Jovanovich, 1985.

McCabe, Katie. "Beyond Cruelty." *The Washingtonian,* February 1990, 73–195.

——. "The Growing Power of the Animal Rights Movement." Paper presented at a meeting of the Board of Governors of the California Biomedical Research Association, July 1987.

——. "Who Will Live, Who Will Die?" *The Washingtonian,* August 1986, 112–57.

Michael, Mike, and Lynda Birke. "Accounting for Animal Experiments: Identity and Disreputable 'Others.'" *Science, Technology, and Human Values* 19 (spring 1994): 189–204.

——. "Enrolling the Core Set: The Case of the Animal Experimentation Controversy." *Social Studies of Science* 24 (1994): 81–95.

Miller, Susan. *The Shame Experience.* Hillsdale, N.J.: The Analytic Press, 1993.

Morris, Aldon D., and Carol McClurg Mueller, eds. *Frontiers in Social Movement Theory.* New Haven, Conn.: Yale University Press, 1992.

Nicoll, Charles S., and Sharon Russell. "Editorial: Analysis of Animal Rights Literature Reveals the Underlying Motives of the Movement: Ammunition for Counter Offensive by Scientists." *Endocrinology* 127 (1990): 985–89.

O'Rourke, P. J. *All the Troubles in the World: The Lighter Side of Famine, Pestilence, Destruction, and Death.* London: Picador, 1995.

Paglia, Camille. *Sex, Art, and American Culture: Essays.* New York: Vintage Books, 1992.

Paris, S. "Letter from the President." *Progress* 1 (1992–1993): 1.

Peck, Peggy. "The New Abolitionists: Animal Rights Terrorists Strike Medicine." *Physicians' Management,* June 1989, 49–68.

"People for the Ethical Treatment of Animals." *Animal Times* 11, no. 1 (spring 1996): 23.

Phillips, Mary T. "Proper Names and the Construction of Biography: The Case of Laboratory Animals." Paper presented at the annual meeting of the American Sociological Association, Cincinnati, Ohio, August 1991.

Phillips, Mary T., and Jeri A. Sechzer. *Animal Research and Ethical Conflict: An Analysis of the Scientific Literature, 1966–1986.* New York: Springer-Verlag, 1989.

Regan, Tom. *The Struggle for Animal Rights.* Clarks Summit, Pa.: International Society for Animal Rights, Inc., 1987.

Richards, Stewart. "Vicarious Suffering, Necessary Pain: Physiological Method in Late Nineteenth-Century Britain." In *Vivisection in Historical Perspective,* edited by Nicholaas A. Rupke, 125–48. London: Croom Helm, 1987.

Rupke, Nicholaas A. "Pro-Vivisection in England in the Early 1880s: Arguments and Motives." In *Vivisection in Historical Perspective,* edited by Nicholaas A. Rupke, 188–208. London: Croom Helm, 1987.

Ryan, Mary P. "Gender and Public Access: Women's Politics in Nineteenth-Century America." In *Habermas and the Public Sphere,* edited by Craig Calhoun, 259–88. Cambridge, Mass.: MIT Press, 1992.

———. *Womanhood in America.* 3d ed. New York: Watts, 1983.

Scheff, Thomas J. *Bloody Revenge: Emotions, Nationalism, and War.* Boulder, Colo.: Westview Press, 1994.

Scheff, Thomas J., and Suzanne M. Retzinger. *Emotions and Violence: Shame and Rage in Destructive Conflicts.* Lexington, Mass.: Lexington Books, 1991.

Seidman, Steven. *Contested Knowledge: Social Theory in the Postmodern Era.* Cambridge, Mass.: Blackwell, 1994.

Serpell, James A. "Pet Keeping in Non-Western Societies: Some Popular Misconceptions." In *Animals and People Sharing the World,* edited by Andrew N. Rowan, 33–52. Hanover, N.H.: University Press of New England, 1988.

Singer, Peter. *Animal Liberation: A New Ethics for Our Treatment of Animals.* New York: Avon Books, 1975.

Snow, David A. "A Dramaturgical Analysis of Movement Accommodation: Building Idiosyncrasy Credit as a Movement Strategy." *Symbolic Interaction* 2 (1979): 23–44.

Snow, David A. E., Burke Rochford Jr., Steven K. Worden, and Robert D. Benford. "Frame Alignment Processes, Micromobilization, and Movement Participation." *American Sociological Review* 51 (1986): 464–81.

Sperling, Susan. *Animal Liberators: Research and Morality.* Berkeley: University of California Press, 1988.

Spradley, James P. *Participant Observation.* Fort Worth, Tex.: Holt, Rinehart and Winston, 1980.

Tannen, Deborah. *You Just Don't Understand: Women and Men in Conversation.* New York: Ballantine Books, 1991.

Thomas, Keith. *Man and the Natural World.* New York: Pantheon, 1983.

Turner, James. *Reckoning with the Beast: Animals, Pain, and Humanity in the Victorian Mind.* Baltimore, Md.: Johns Hopkins University Press, 1980.

Turner, Ralph. "The Real Self: From Institution to Impulse." *American Journal of Sociology* 81 (1976): 989–1016.

"What Humans Owe to Animals." *The Economist,* August 19, 1995.

White, Robert J. "The Facts About Animal Research." *Reader's Digest,* March 1988, 127–32.

Wurmser, Léon. *The Mask of Shame.* Baltimore, Md.: Johns Hopkins University Press, 1981.

Zussman, Robert. *Intensive Care: Medical Ethics and the Medical Profession.* Chicago: University of Chicago Press, 1992.

Index

Adams, Carol, 43
administrators, research: middle-level
    (*see* Institutional Animal Care and
    Use Committee; veterinarians:
    laboratory); senior (*see* animal
    researchers)
African Americans, 3, 150–51, 182. *See
    also* civil rights movement
ALF. *See* Animal Liberation Front
AMA (American Medical Associa-
    tion), 46, 163–64
American Association for Accredita-
    tion of Laboratory Animal Care,
    176
American Diabetes Association, 73,
    119
American Medical Association
    (AMA), 46, 163–64
American Psychological Association,
    78–79
Americans for Medical Progress, 166
Amnesty International, 21, 71
Amory, Cleveland, 58
anger: acceptable, 132–34; men's, 12;
    shame about, 5. *See also* animal
    rights activist(s): men; Singer, Peter
Animal Legal Defense Fund, 41
Animal Liberation Front (ALF), 38,
    40, 66, 133–44, 166–67

animal protection, 28; definition of,
    205n; before the eighteenth cen-
    tury, 31–33; in the nineteenth cen-
    tury, 33–36; in the 1950s, 36–38;
    recent history of, 38–44 (*see also* an-
    imal research); symbolic meaning
    of, 9
animal protection ordinances. *See* ani-
    mal protection regulations
animal protection organizations. *See*
    animal rights organizations; animal
    welfare organizations
animal protection regulations: animal
    rights activists' attitude toward, 81,
    99, 188; history of, 47–49, 50; prob-
    lems enforcing, 30, 173–88; viola-
    tions of, 25–26, 39–40, 115–16,
    121, 177, 179–80, 184–85, 187–88
animal research: animal rights activ-
    ists' criticisms of, 2, 85–86, 92–94,
    100–101; and early experimenters,
    44; in the nineteenth century, 45–
    46; recent history of, 46–50; in the
    Renaissance, 44; in the seventeenth
    and eighteenth centuries, 44–45
animal researchers: African Ameri-
    cans and, 182; age of, 77; animal
    caretakers and, 174, 175, 182–85,
    187; becoming involved in the con-